Improve Your Social Skills

How to Improve Conversations, Stop People Pleasing and Improve Your People Skills

Legal Notice:

Disclaimer Notice:

Please note the information contained within this document is for educational and entertainment purposes only. Every attempt has been made to provide accurate, up to date and reliable complete information. No warranties of any kind are expressed or implied. Readers acknowledge that the author is not engaging in the rendering of legal, financial, medical or professional advice. The content of this book has been derived from various sources. Please consult a licensed professional before attempting any techniques outlined in this book.

By reading this document, the reader agrees that under no circumstances are is the author responsible for any losses, direct or indirect, which are incurred as a result of the use of information contained within this document, including, but not limited to, —errors, omissions, or inaccuracies.

Table of Contents

Introduction

A guy is at a party. He knows almost nobody there, so he stays in one corner, listening to other people's conversations, and browsing social media on his phone. After a while, a small group comes next to him, and he pays attention to them. They are talking about how much they loved the last *Star Trek* movie. Our protagonist knows about it; in fact, he watched it last night. He wants to make a move by entering the conversation and perhaps making some friends. But something inside him grabs him, holds him back, and forces him to stay put. After a while, they change the subject, and the opportunity is lost forever.

Perhaps you didn't exactly recognize yourself in the above example (maybe you aren't fond of parties or *Star Trek* movies). However, if you have ever felt that grasp in your chest, and that voice in your head that says "they will laugh at me", then this book is for you.

In clear and simple steps, we are going to tackle how to make new friends, maintain friendships, and become a better person. I will be with you along the ride and will tell you my experiences with anxiety and social awkwardness. For this I have a newsletter you can signup to at http://jen.green for us to keep in touch with each other. You will see that, although I am now writing a book about the subject, I was once just like you. You will also learn how to detect toxic people in your life and how to avoid them.

This book is not just focused on learning to identify your problem when it comes to social skills, but also on improving. This book is aimed at those that want a change in their lives, that want to focus and, finally and after a lot of practice and work, correct their problems. This is extremely important, and it will require the reader (that is: you) to put their focus on a goal and achieve it.

If you are this type of person, welcome to my book. The road ahead will be hard, but it will all be worth it.

For now, all I can say is…

Breath.

Okay?

Let's do it.

Chapter 1

What are Social Skills?

My old teacher once told me: "Social skills are what separate us from animals". I always thought it was a weird saying, even before I understood precisely what social skills were. When I was a kid, I didn't have many friends, and my parents were worried that there might be something wrong with me. They tried absolutely everything: organizing parties at home, inviting the other kids at school to a playdate - you name it. But nothing worked; I didn't know what to do when I was in a conversation with someone. I was timid, so that didn't help either.

My parents, willing to do anything to improve my life at school and in general, brought home a small puppy. I could name it whatever I wanted, and since for some reason the puppy loved to munch on rocks, I decided to take the easy way out and call it Rocks. It was love at first sight. Rocks and I were always together; he would come with me to the doctor, and even waited for me outside my school. And the dog became my very best, and at that time, only friend.

I would go on walks with him and tell him things that

happened at school that day, and I promise you - Rocks understood every single word that I said. I don't have any tangible proof, but he did. He was loyal, friendly and the very definition of a "good boy". If you ever looked up "good boy" in a dictionary, you would have found a picture of Rocks smiling at you.

Close to where I lived, there was a park where kids had fun and played soccer. I always watched them from a distance, since I didn't know anybody. I always wanted to play with them, or at least talk to them, but I was too shy. What could I tell them? They seemed "cool", while I didn't have much to talk about (or at least, that's what I thought at the time). But Rocks, being the kind of friend that he was, knew exactly what to do. One day, like always, we went to the park and the kids were there having fun. Rocks decided that it was time for me to meet other people, so he headed towards them, grabbed the ball with his mouth, and brought it to me.

The kids enjoyed that and came running behind Rocks. When they saw that I was there alone, the kids decided to invite me to play with them. Rocks watched from the side, wiggling his tail every time I touched the ball. When I scored a goal (by all accounts a real miracle and the definite proof of the existence of superior beings, since I barely knew the rules), he came close and licked my face. After that, the kids and I started to become friends. We started to meet there every Sunday to play football, and then, when one of them got a Sega Genesis, we spent hours in his house playing video games. I knew some of them from school, but two or three were their cousins or older kids. When they heard the news, my parents were excited. Finally, I had met new people! And it was all thanks to Rocks.

The purpose of this book, of course, isn't to tell you that you should adopt a dog, or tell you about the adventures of Rocks, but to teach you about social skills. Of course, in the story, we touched on one factor - the ability to make friends and interact with society.

If we go by the scientific definition, we could say that social skills are any competence or ability that allow communication and interaction with the rest of the world. The basis of society lies in this interaction. We agree that there are things that we do or don't do because there are social, often unspoken rules regarding how to act in a specific situation. If you read it like this, it doesn't define what it means, but during this book, you will understand it more clearly.

Social skills, when it comes to socialization, are called **interpersonal skills**. These skills are essential to relate to other people because these are interpersonal (that means, between two or more people) acts that a person uses to interact with others.

Interpersonal skills will be explained in full in the following chapter, but the essential skills are the following:

- Active listening

- Delegation

- Leadership

Among many others. If you want to understand and learn about them, jump to the following chapter.

I mentioned that social skills are the tools that we have to communicate with one another, and you might think that it only involves speech, but you would be wrong. Social skills include so much more, like:

- Mentoring

- Persuasion

- Service Orientation

- Social Perceptiveness

- Coordination

- Negotiation

All these skills can be learned and improved over time, and the only way to really do that is to put your mind to it. I used to be a timid kid with no friends. Now, I can say that my life is entirely different. And yes, you might say that it was all thanks to Rocks, but the truth is, he saw the potential in me, just like I see the potential in you. You have what it takes to be the leader of a group and gain acceptance and recognition from your peers.

Let's start with the basics: What do you consider a friend? What is the definition of friendship for you?

If your answer is to have someone by your side no matter what, who you can tell all your secrets to and that won't back down or leave you alone, you are correct. Friendships shape us in ways that we cannot fully comprehend, and social skills are our tool for that.

Mentoring, for example, is the ability to teach other people how to perform a task. We can teach or coach mentorees or other people on a particular skill, and facilitate their growth by sharing our resources and networks. We can also focus on our mentoree's development, helping they grow beyond what is expected of them. This, in general terms, is mentoring. However, it is so much more than this.

It is the ability that we humans have to be there when someone falls and help him get back up. Do you have an older or younger sibling? If you do, you will see that you tend to help him when he has problems at school, or when he is stuck at a particularly hard level on a video game. It is something that we cannot control; we go and teach them how to deal with problems in life. That's mentoring applied to real life and not to a business setting, and it is something that we sometimes do unconsciously. We do it because "it is the right thing to do".

Persuasion, for example, is the social skill where the following great saying applies:

"With great power comes great responsibility"

It is the ability to convince others of your point of view or to do something for you. Too much of this, and you will end up becoming a manipulative person. Striking that balance is quite hard, and it is something that sadly, not many people manage to master. They just manipulate people for their own benefit, making them toxic people.

But persuasive people have a secret weapon, and that is that they are really likable because they aren't just selling you an idea, they are also making you happily buy into it. They tend to connect with people easily because they know what to say to make the other person accept them. They avoid arguments without meaning, and they always keep in mind that they are talking to a person, not an opponent or an objective.

Persuasive people don't push their ideas. They present the facts (or in some cases, their version of the facts) and let you make a decision. They also use positive body language (more on this later), and they are clear and concise, so they are straight to the point when presenting their ideas and opinions.

They are quite skilled in several topics and subjects, and they have service orientation, which is the desire and ability to anticipate the needs of their audience. So, if they know that they are presenting an idea that the group doesn't like, they will do it thinking about the future needs of everyone in that group. This, in turn, means that their idea is easily accepted.

Coordination and negotiation are perfect if you want to master your social skills since these two skills are great in both a business setting and your everyday life. Coordination is the ability to coordinate two or more groups to do something together, and it goes perfectly with teamwork. In fact, without coordination, you wouldn't have sports teams or any sort of social group activity.

Negotiation, on the other hand, is the ability to manage several points of view to reach common ground. You can see this in politicians and leaders everywhere. If they have a complicated situation, they propose an idea or a plan, listen to the debate that it generates, and then, from all the different points of view, they reach a conclusion that is the sum of all the opinions. As you can see, this is perfect for any relationship, since you will be negotiating even the smallest things, like which movie to watch tonight, to bigger and more important things, like where to go on vacation this year.

Chapter 2

Interpersonal Skills

In the previous section, I talked a little about interpersonal skills and mentioned a few of them. In this chapter, we will explore them in more depth.

The term "interpersonal skills" refers to character traits possessed by an individual that cannot be learned in a classroom, like an essential date in history or maths, although there are scientific studies that indicate that early interaction with other kids of the same age has an enormous influence in the development of a human being. When it comes to job hunting, interpersonal skills are extremely important, since the employees that have excellent interpersonal skills are more inclined to project a positive attitude and find solutions to any kind of problem that may arise, whereas employees that lack this kind of skill are often unproductive when there is a problem or not strictly adhering to deadlines.

Hollywood and television, in general, have shown us characters that are socially awkward time and time again, and everybody likes them, despite their failings and problems. Take for example Benedict Cumberbatch's version of Sherlock Holmes for the BBC show of the same name: he doesn't know how to interact with his family or friends (for example, his relationship with Martin Freeman's John Watson is a perfect representation of his lack of social skills), and, at the end of the day, everything goes according to his plan, the world is saved, and everything is great. His problems are ignored for a moment, and then, come the next episode, he's back to being weird around people. This kind of representation in the media encourages the idea that socially awkward people have absolutely no need to change or improve because in the end, it doesn't really matter and people will still put up with their problems. While I do love the series and Mr. Cumberbatch's acting, I have to say that it isn't a good representation of what a socially awkward person can, or should do.

Let's remember that when we talk about interpersonal skills, we are talking about the knowledge one might have about social customs and expectations, and how to react to other people's actions and adjust accordingly. Some people describe these sort of skills as another form of intelligence called social intelligence. It relies on paying particular attention to the speech and actions of other people and interpreting it correctly before forming a response. In other words, it is the ability to comprehend and understand what the rest of the world is saying or why it is acting like it is, and then adapting, and adjusting our behavior to it. For example: If you see someone crying, you probably won't talk to that person with a smile on your face, or with an upbeat attitude, at least until you get the full facts and understand why that person is crying. While these types of skills are partly based on instincts and personality, they can also be developed with knowledge, self-consciousness and life experiences.

Now, let's tackle several examples, expand, and explain each one of these interpersonal skills so we can see how to apply those in both personal and business settings:

Emotional intelligence

This refers to the ability to be aware of your own emotions and keep them under control. Have you ever met someone who, at the first sign of discomfort or conflict, starts going on and on about how the world or people hate him? This is a perfect example of someone who doesn't have an excellent grasp on his emotions and cannot navigate social situations easily.

This is quite an important skill to have, and it can be learned quickly in the course of your life. When you are looking for a new job or work in an office, employers will always pay attention to your attitude when dealing with frustration. If you don't keep your emotions in check, people will believe – perhaps wrongly - that they can't trust you in an emergency or when you have to work overtime to finish a deadline. Being able to stay calm and to keep your emotions under control is invaluable in any workplace, no matter the position. Would you prefer to work with a boss who is calm or someone who decides that the best way to approach a problem is to shout? The answer is simple and quite obvious.

In the same vein, if you always blame all your fallings on external problems or other coworkers, you will create a hostile working environment because your co-workers or employees will begin to avoid responsibility, and that, in the long run, is ultimately a death blow to the aspirations of any company.

Communication

"Express your problems, express your ideas, and express your feelings". This mantra was written in the office where I got my first job. I was almost 20, had basically no experience (it was an accounting job), and I took the mantra to heart. Motivated by this saying, I started gaining friends and experience, and almost a year after I started working there, I got a promotion and more significant responsibilities.

This is a mantra that you can use and apply to your life: Does the topic that you are discussing with someone bother you? Say it. Do you have a better idea than the one that is currently being discussed in the meeting? Say it. Do you have feelings for someone? Say it.

Yes, I know, it might be easy to say, but the truth is, if

you are trying to progress in the workplace, you have to put yourself out there. Your fear of a possible rejection is holding you back in ways that I cannot express. And if they say no, or they believe that your idea isn't that great, well, what do you lose? Nothing will happen, and, in an office setting, your input will be appreciated, because it means that you are proactive and always have the company in mind. This, of course, applies to the workplace, but your personal life can be affected too. What about asking that person out? What's the worst that can happen? They say no, and both of you continue with your life. See? It isn't that bad.

Reliability

There is an emergency at your office. The reports that have to be delivered to the client aren't done, and the deadline is tomorrow. Your boss knows that this is a big problem, and asks the employees to stay overtime, all expenses paid. These reports are critical, and the company's future depends on them. What do you do?

If your first answer is to say no and go home, then you might not be as reliable as your company needs you to be, or perhaps you don't like the job, which is something that you can explore by yourself. Reliability is a skill that encapsulates your integrity and your work ethic to finish and always take the extra step to see things through to the end. If your bosses see that when there is a problem or emergency, they can rely on your presence and work ethic, your actions will have a profound impact on that company, especially when it is time to do the annual performance review. And, it goes without saying that if you prove yourself to be reliable, your bosses will be more inclined to support you when you wish to change jobs.

Reliability can not only be used in a work-related setting. For example, let's say that your friend has a really bad breakup with her boyfriend. She calls you one day to see if you want to join her to grab some coffee and help her get her mind off the breakup. You say no because you have other things to do. Then, a day later, she calls you again asking if you want to go somewhere else. She really needs your company. However, you say no again. And so on and so forth. After a while, she doesn't call you anymore and avoids responding to your texts. What happened is that she realized that you aren't reliable, since every time she calls you to meet up, you already have plans. If you want to create a strong bond with your friends, you have to dedicate enough time to allow the relationship to grow. After creating a friendship, it's not as simple as hoping for the best for it. A true bond is basically like a flower; if you don't dedicate enough time to take care of it, it will wither and die. You don't want that.

Leadership

You will use this interpersonal skill more in your job than in your day-to-day life, but the benefits of learning and knowing when to use it will help you project a strong sense of security that will improve your life.

In your work environment, having the leadership skill under your belt is what separates you from your peers. We mentioned that reliability would have a strong impact on your annual performance review, but leadership too. Your employers are always looking for capable and motivated workers, especially those who can inspire others and lead the way when it is time to get work done.

However, leadership doesn't just mean ordering people to do a certain task, or write down an operational plan for the future of the company. It also involves helping your employees to improve themselves, get the best out of them and their work, and make them feel valuable by helping them create important contributions to the organization. If you ever come across a leader who exhibits these skills, you will immediately see the effect that they have on everybody around them. In my experience, the best way to get things done at the company level is to hire and find these people, so that is why it is a desirable skill to have.

Positivity

Ah, positivity. This is definitely something that more people should focus on, especially when we see how things are doing around the world. Positivity not only involves looking at a glass half full; it is a way of thinking and living that involves absolutely every facet of your life, and I can show you how to think more positively.

When something bad happens in your life or in the life of those around you, what is your immediate reaction? To cry? To get angry? If you decide to look on the bright side of the situation, and how to solve it, congratulations, you are a natural optimist and an overall positive person.

Positivity is a way of thinking that allows one to tackle a problem and deal with it the best way possible. It is finding a solution in the most reliable and fastest way possible. Then, after the problem is solved and everything is done, you can sit down and see what the mistake was. However, always keep in mind that no matter how big the problem might seem, there is always light at the end of the tunnel. Perhaps you will have to make sacrifices to reach that goal, or perhaps you will have to work overtime, but you will ultimately reach it.

Training to think more positively about life is something that should be done every day. It should not only be done when disaster strikes but with small things too. For example, if it is raining and you forgot your umbrella, smile and try your best not to get wet. In time, you will learn to always bring it in case it rains, and you will be sure to always check the weather forecast before going outside. Or if you see that you don't have enough money for the lunch you were planning, smile and pick a cheaper one. Positivity is a way to say to the universe, "No matter what you are sending me, I will deal with it and triumph over any and all problems that arise in my life."

A long time ago, my company had a special arrangement with the local hospital where we could volunteer and spend a day with sick kids. If you ever have the possibility to do it, I would highly suggest it, unless it triggers bad memories for you, as I know it is not easy to watch and talk to kids that know that their diseases are terminal. I spent my entire day talking to a kid named David who knew that he had less than four months to live. In that situation, it would be absolutely normal and understandable if he were angry at the world, at life, or at his disease. However, it was quite the contrary, as David was constantly smiling and he told me that he decided to deal with whatever life he has left with a smile and a positive attitude.

His mother told me that David's positivity improved his health, and while it didn't completely cure him (nothing short of a miracle would do that), it extended his prognosis. I left that day thinking that positivity is the secret tool against every possible problem that we might have in our lives. Of course, it is not a magical cure, or anything close to that, but it can definitely improve how we deal with our lives. Positivity is such a fantastic skill to have in people around you because it allows not just you, but also the people you love to see the best in any given situation. In a work environment, this is a skill that elevates a company. If you have a management position, your employees will absolutely adore if you radiate positivity in every action that you take. It is better to be positive and deal with whatever might happen than being pessimistic and bringing everyone around you down.

Negotiation

The act of negotiating is crucial for whatever enterprise you want to follow later in your life or career, and it is the basis of a strong and reliable friendship. It is not just the act of selling or buying goods, but it is also any sort of interaction where two or more people try to reach common ground after engaging in a discussion. In the workplace, the art of negotiating happens at all times, from trying to get a salary raise, to telling your coworker if he can turn the volume down on his cellphone down so you can concentrate. It happens in ways that we don't see or pay attention to.

However, in a relationship, negotiating is used in a more obvious way. For example, if you both want to go out to the theatre that week, you have to negotiate which movie you will see, or what menu will you order at dinner after the movie. The clearer way to deal with this is quite simple: one for you, one for them. If this week you get to see "Alvin and the Chipmunks" (when you wanted to see "Captain Marvel"), you can pick the menu, and next week, the roles will be reversed.

If you are in a large group of people, the best way is a democracy: vote for whatever plan you want to have that night. If there's a majority, then you have your choice. With my group of friends, if there's a draw, we flip a coin. Chances are that one of the two plans will be decided, and everybody's happy because they know that next week, they get to decide.

However, if your plan failed to get enough votes, don't be pessimistic, as that may lead to your plan in the future not earning the support it needs or deserves.

Feedback

Feedback isn't just the opinion or critique a coworker can give you (or bosses when it is time for the annual performance review), but also when friends and family give us their opinion.

It hurts our ego when something that we are sure we are doing correctly turns out to be wrong. We believed that we were doing it really well, but the reality is, it wasn't good enough. When people tell us that, we have to keep an open mind and understand that most of the time, they are saying it because they want us to do better, work to the full extent of our abilities, and strive to greater things. Yes, sometimes, they are doing it because they are jealous of our success or interests, so the key is to differentiate between opinions that are born from malice and selfishness and those born out of pure interest in our improvement.

If we want to be professional (and most of all, be perceived as such), we need to train our mindset to suppress our ego down to manageable levels and accept feedback. We can then apply whatever critique they might have of our abilities or attitudes and use it to improve our understanding of the world and become better people.

When the critique comes from someone close to us, the process is a bit different, because the critique, in its very nature, is different. Receiving feedback from our bosses or parents is not the same thing. The latter do it because they have an emotional bond with us, and it pains them to see us failing or not reaching our full potential.

Always be aware of what and who is telling us how to improve, and review the emotional context of each of them. In time, you will learn to process and use this feedback to create the best possible version of yourself.

When it is your turn to apply feedback to someone you love or care about, always be aware of the emotional state of that person. If your feedback is going to be negative, always do it with tact and in a private setting. Never offer feedback when you are in public. Always offer to do it somewhere that is quiet and where you are alone. This way, you will ensure that both of you have privacy and external factors won't interfere with your talk. This same suggestion applies at the professional level: never do it in front of your other employees, because you put the other person at a disadvantage since they cannot reply to you without undermining your position.

Empathy

Empathy, just like positivity, is something that we could use more of. It is the connection that we create with someone who doesn't have the same possibilities as us or is having a bad time. It is the ability to lend a hand because we understand that it is the right thing to do. Empathy is also the skill that makes us remain silent when someone doesn't feel great and just wants to vent or cry on our shoulders. It is, in other words, to put ourselves in their shoes.

My father always said that empathy is one of those skills that he believed society in general had and which manifests itself in special situations. For example, every time a disaster hits, whether manmade or natural, you see hundreds or even thousands of people helping, and even sometimes putting their own lives at risk in order to lend a hand and help those in need. I still believe that my father was right.

When it comes to empathy in a business setting, it can be displayed in various ways. A coworker could ask you for advice because they are experiencing problems with their boss, or to cover for someone when they have to go to the doctor to get their annual checkup. And if you have a career in teaching, empathy goes a long way towards helping your students learn, because teaching is far more than just reciting things from memory. Perhaps some kids are having a rough time at home, so you could adapt your teaching to help that class.

On a personal level, empathy is one of the cornerstones of a strong and secure relationship. You cannot begin to create a relationship unless you have empathy. This skill, along with others, creates feedback between you and other people. If you treat people correctly, they will treat you the same in return. Empathy enables to open your feelings and your true self to others, and they will accept you for it. It is a skill that you have to try developing every day.

Teamwork

Both in the workplace and in your interactions with the rest of the world, teamwork is a great interpersonal skill to master. The benefits are far-reaching and will improve any relationship that you want to build.

In this book, we talk about how to get new friends, especially in a setting like a new job or living in another city, but in order to create a bond between you and people, the best way is to do teamwork-related activities. There is a current trend among companies to take employees to an escape room game. This is a great idea because you will be locked up (safely, of course) in a thematic room and you have to find clues and work your way out in a certain amount of time. The pressure of the clock ticking is a great motivator for groups to delegate activities and work towards a common goal, which in this case, is to escape the room.

These activities basically serve as training to work towards a goal when a deadline is close by. You will quickly learn to delegate activities and to trust your partners to do a great job. Teamwork not only helps you in your career but also in relationships, as it is a skill that will help you form strong connections with people. It is often said that friendship proves itself when you work towards a common goal.

Let me tell you a story that will illustrate this point. I always wanted to go to Europe for a trip, and my closest friend was in the same situation as me. So, we decided to plan a trip together. We set ourselves a goal; we agreed that in three years, we would be there. Then, we realized that the best way to focus on it was to separate it into smaller tasks. These tasks included booking out hotels and plane tickets, finding out the best places to go, plan activities, create a guide of things to see, and particularly save enough money to do all the things that we wanted to do. We created a shared bank account, and every month, we worked a few overtime hours, with the extra money going directly into that account. We did it with enough planning and trust in each other that when the time came, we didn't have to ask the other if he had done his work. He did, and of course, I did all the tasks that I was assigned to do. After several months of planning, and particularly fantastic teamwork, we spent an incredible month in Spain, France, and Germany, and I can say, without any doubt, that our friendship grew stronger thanks to it.

Active Listening

This is a secret that every proved politician and successful businessman has mastered. It is impossible to reach higher spheres of power without this skill, and this is the most important skill to learn. If you can master it, then, as my brother says, the sky is the limit.

Have you ever been to a business convention and seen the speaker listen to every single question asked, and that actually dealt with each one of them personally? This is Active Listening. It is paying attention to what they say, how they say it, and offering the best possible response. This, of course, doesn't mean lying or hiding the truth, but clearly understanding the conflict or problem.

If you work in the service industry, you will see that when a customer comes to you with a complaint, they expect you to pay attention to them and solve the problem. Active listening, in this case, is to see where you can help, what the best solution to reach is and what your abilities are. A strong listening ability is beneficial not just in work-related activities but also in your daily life.

We mentioned empathy and optimism, and while they are important, if you don't practice your active listening, they won't be as effective as possible. Listen and pay attention to how and why they are asking this from you because it will be essential in the future.

Politicians, no matter their color or political stance, always use this to get citizens to vote for them. If you ever meet a politician, you will see that they watch every person in their eyes, have their backs straight, and are very careful with their answers. The most successful CEOs and technological gurus (Elon Musk, Steve Jobs, Bill Gates, Jeff Bezos, etc) are all like this. Just watch one of their interviews, and you will see that their answers are concise, direct, and straight to the point. Also, active listening is always the tool used to innovate or push a new product on the market.

Chapter 3

Pleasing People (and How to Stop)

We all want to be loved. That's the truth behind most of our actions. If we go to a soccer match with our friends, even if we don't like sports, we might be doing it to spend time with them, trying to find new common ground or a new hobby to enjoy together. But the truth is, behind all of this, we do it to be loved. This is not a bad thing at all, and it is good to strike a balance. However, in reality, most people who lack social skills try to overcompensate by pleasing everybody they meet.

You might have done it without realizing. You try to avoid arguments or conflicts, and when you are dragged into one, you lower your head (metaphorically) and lose the battle. You try to do your best to get away from the argument by basically agreeing with the other person, even if, deep inside, you don't agree with his opinion or actions. And this, after a while, becomes a problem. You decide to do or act in a certain way, just because you didn't say "no" when the time came. And, as bad as this might sound, some people will take advantage of this:

after all, you won't say no, even if you hate what you are doing.

This eagerness to say yes and please everybody comes from self-esteem and worth issues. We don't feel like we are worth the attention because we feel like we are just not good enough. So, we compensate and say yes. We wrongly believe that this will help us get new friends and be loved. Other people have a history of maltreatment, and after a while, perhaps unconsciously, they decide that their best shot at being loved and be treated better was to please the rest of the world. Over time, this ends up becoming a way of life.

They will tell you that they are "kind" or that they want to avoid being selfish. Their intentions might be good, but the root is that they try to please someone under the disguise of "being a good person". This might be a severe problem, and it is a habit that is quite hard to break from. But don't worry. That's why I'm here.

Let me give you an example of a situation, and let's then analyze what might be the problem:

John works until 6 pm every day at a software company. He gets home after a rough day, and his roommate, Mike, is in the living room, playing video games. The entire house is a mess, and it was Mike's turn to clean up. But, instead of confronting him, John decides to do it himself. He doesn't want to make any problems, so he starts cleaning up. Dinner arrives, and John is hungry. But Mike is still in the living room and hasn't moved an inch. So John makes dinner for both of them. He goes to bed, and then, day after day, this continues. Rinse and repeat.

While this is a straightforward example, it might be all too familiar for you. We all have done this once or twice; we decided to do it ourselves because we didn't want to bother the rest, and in the end, ended up doing everything and neglect our own health.

Let's talk about what John did (and what Mike didn't):

John felt responsible for how Mike felt, because he was having fun playing video games, and everybody needs a bit of rest sometimes. But while it is healthy to recognize how your behavior affects and influences people around you, thinking (or even worse, believing) that you and you alone have the power to make someone happy is a big problem. It is not up to you (or John, in this case) to be in charge of other people's emotions. Obviously, like all the things that we are going to talk about in this book (and it is an advice that you can apply to the rest of your life), the most important thing is to strike a balance between both extremes.

Awkward people tend to often apologize, and this sometimes annoys their family and friends. This is something that is quite common with most people, and I am sure that you found yourself in this situation quite often. But the reality is that sometimes, we do it because we are told that whatever we do, we are in the wrong. Perhaps they do it without knowing that they are doing it, but their negative comments hurt us in a way that we don't fully understand until we are of a certain age. Negative comments stay ingrained in our brain and conscience, and we tend to listen to that negativity when we are in doubt about choices in our lives. These kind of decisions aren't just the big ones, like buying a house, having kids, changing jobs, etc., but even the smallest decisions, like going to McDonald's, meeting someone for a coffee, getting a new pair of shoes, etc. The problem with these kind of voices is that when something wrong actually happens (the McDonalds menu upset your stomach, or the house that you bought has plumbing problems), it reinforces the idea that the choice that we made was the wrong one, and that we shouldn't have bothered with it, and we end up thinking that our parents or friends were right.

If you find yourself in this kind of situation, the one advice that I can give you is to try to calm down and relax for a while. I know, this is quite a tall order, and it is difficult to do, but the truth is that no matter what situation you are in, your primary concern should be yourself and your loved ones. If anything is happening, nothing will be gained by being negative, shouting that people were right, or that you should haven't done it. First, try to solve whatever problem you might have, and then, only then, when the problem is fixed or is at least headed that way, try to think about the mistakes that you made. Perhaps you shouldn't have eaten a Big Mac because you know that you have a weak stomach, or maybe you should have checked out the plumbing before getting a loan to buy that house. All these small exercises will help you create a better sense of your limitations and understandings. This, in turn, will help you feel confident and change your life. This may not happen right away, but in time, it will change.

When you work in an office, or you have a certain amount of friends and relationships, you will start to see that sometimes, you might feel like you don't want to see anybody. Perhaps your co-worker, a guy who is great and that you like to be around, invites you to an after-office party, and you feel compelled to go. After all, you enjoy talking to him. But something is wrong that day. You woke up without any interest in going to a party, and your plan includes staying at home and watching a movie or ordering a pizza and reading a book. If you are a people pleaser, you will feel compelled to go, even if you don't want to. Why do we do this? The reasons are obvious - we feel like if we don't go, people will stop talking to us. It's already hard enough to make friends, and it will be harder if we lose the few that we already have. So, we go, but every minute that we spend in that party watching people have fun, we think that we would rather be at home or somewhere else. It is not like it is not a good party or anything like that, but just the simple fact that we would be enjoying ourselves far more elsewhere.

This is quite normal, and if you ever feel like this, don't think for one second that you are in the wrong. Sometimes, you need a bit of space and time to enjoy yourself. Think about the kind of activities that you do, or how you spend your week - how much time do you dedicate to pleasure? Are you doing anything that you don't enjoy because you feel like it is what people expect from you? If the answer is yes, it is a sign that you might be a people pleaser, and that you are ignoring your health just because people think that you have to do something, like going out for drinks every day, or spending weekends with your coworkers, etc.

It is reasonable to want to leave your work-related relationships at work, and to prefer spending time alone. The best way to deal with this is to talk to your co-workers and explain to them that you have other plans on that day. Keep your tone calm and firm, because people will sense security and take you seriously. This is quite important, so it is something that must be practiced every day. After a while, you will start doing it naturally. If your partners or friends don't like your suggestion, remain firm and don't be afraid of saying no. They won't stop loving you if you decide to skip an after-office party, and if they do, they are the sort of people that you don't want around anyway.

But let's assume that your friends or partners don't like the idea that you stopped going to birthday parties, and they tell you that they are angry. Or maybe they don't tell you, but they start treating you differently or speaking behind your back. While their anger is something that you can't control and you can only be yourself, you might be feeling guilty or uncomfortable. But there is one small piece of advice my mother once told me - just because someone is mad at you, it doesn't necessarily mean that you did anything wrong. So, in this situation, you have to understand (and write down the words if you have to) that sometimes, you can't control how people feel about your actions. And guess what? That is okay. You can't control everything, and never compromise your values (especially if it means doing something that you don't want to do) just because people have expressed anger towards you.

Friday comes, and in an almost vain attempt, they insist, wanting to see if you changed your opinion, and after a week of hearing their complains because you don't like going out with them, you decide, almost without knowing, that you will go. Your co-workers can't understand it, but they happily accept you among them. They believe that you weren't sure about coming, and had to think about it. But the truth is, you did it just to get them off your back. At the bar, they drink, and like most people, they start shouting and being loud after a couple of beers. You don't drink, but you think that if you don't act like them, people will start complaining. So you shout just like them, even if deep inside, you know it is wrong. And while you are screaming and being a nuisance (because they are doing it too), someone says that you are funny. That compliment that came out of nowhere makes you feel loved, and they seem to enjoy the "new you". Perhaps it wasn't that bad of an idea to act this way.

I understand what you are thinking: "What is the problem of showing other people a different side of your personality?", and I agree, there's no problem with that. On the contrary, it is common sense: you wouldn't act the same way with your boss as you would with your family and friends. But that doesn't mean that you have to change your entire personality just to fit in. It is one thing to adapt, but another thing entirely to change your entire self to be "one of the guys". In the search for friends or significant others, don't lose sight of your personality, because when you start doing so, you will start losing your true self, and that is a shame. Shape up your character, adapt, but don't lose your values.

Compliments, on the other hand, can be addictive. Apparently, it goes without saying that receiving encouraging words from partners or family members is an awesome feeling, especially when it comes out of nowhere. People pleasers tend to depend on validation, and that's where it might go wrong since they start to associate validation or compliments with self-worth. If that happens to you, you might have a problem. For example, what happens when you stop getting that validation? Perhaps you stopped doing a good job, or they just stopped giving you attention. If your image or self-worth is caused and affected entirely by what other people think about you, you will start to associate happiness with their compliments. Learn to understand your limits and take care of your image.

One of the social skills vital to forming healthy and long-standing relationships is something that most people struggle with - being honest and admitting when your feelings are hurt. Yes, however strange this might sound, people struggle with this because sometimes, we are raised to believe that our opinions aren't that important, or that we have to "man up" and "deal with it", no matter how toxic this can be. But the pillar of forming a lasting and meaningful relationship with anybody is to speak up and admit that your feelings were hurt. No matter how stupid it might look to you, or however small you might think the problem is, if you don't do it and just bottle up, or even worse, deny it, the relationships that you create will always stay superficial.

Believe me when I say this, as I'm talking from experience. In the past, I used to feel like I couldn't trust the people around me. I used to think that, I couldn't share any problems or concerns that I might have with them. Sure, I had friends, but I always kept a somewhat safe distance between my feelings or problems and them, even when they started to trust me with their most important secrets. I felt like they would laugh at my questions, or that they might think that they weren't that important, (and perhaps they weren't, but for me, they felt like they were) until a couple of years ago when I got a job in a new city. I moved, started at a new office, at a position that I was way under qualified for (but with a fantastic salary), and felt utterly lost. Then, my mind did absolute wonders: I felt like if I made one mistake, I would have to quit right there, because the pressure was too high, and I really needed the money. I couldn't ask for help in the new office, because I didn't want to look like how I felt - a con man.

Of course, I wrongly decided that I should just deal with it and face my problems. But after a small, minor complaint from a customer, I couldn't deal with it and went to the bathroom to cry. I felt lost, absolutely overwhelmed and utterly alone in this new city where I didn't know anybody. Somehow, and if I may get a little deep, I will say that it was thanks to the spirit of Rocks that my friend back home sent me a message asking me how I felt at my new job. I couldn't hide it anymore, so I called him and told him everything I felt. After months of hiding my emotions, I was suddenly talking about my feelings. My friend, bless him, was shocked. He didn't expect it. So, he took a bus that very same afternoon and came to see me. We spent a week together, and after talking for hours, he went back. Of course, we still keep in touch, but now it's more honest from my side. I talk to him almost every day, and we both felt like our friendship grew stronger thanks to that incident. Trust your friends. Talk to them. Don't make the same mistake as me. Don't wait until you can't deal with it. Be honest. Be open. True friendship lies behind that door.

We talked about what defines a people pleaser, and we also spoke a little about what we can do to avoid being one of them. But let's talk about how to break free from that habit. This is quite a lengthy process, and if you ever feel like you can't do it by yourself, you can always seek professional help. A therapist might help you build the necessary mental strength to be able to create the kind of life that you want to have.

Let's start with the most basic advice that I can give you - try to start saying no to small things. And with that, I mean really small things. For example, start by saying no to eating a specific dish just because everybody is ordering it. Order whatever you want to eat. Or, for example, express your opinion about something straightforward, like a movie, or a book, nothing life-changing. Keep doing it for a while, and practice it every day. In time, you will have the necessary strength and mental fortitude to tackle significant discussions.

Earlier, we touched on validation; how it is essential to everybody, and how it may lead to being a people pleaser. But let's talk about how to fight the feeling to need that validation, or rather, that confirmation that you are worthy. In my experience, I found that the best way to combat this kind of habit is to build up what makes you feel happy or good. The idea behind this is quite simple: if you feel happy doing whatever you love doing, such as acting on stage, for example, do it. You don't need others to make you feel great. They just add to your happiness or self-worth. The best way to realize this is to hang around people who make you feel great because they like you just the way you are. They don't try to force their views onto you or change the way you are. They accept you, with all your faults and achievements. They are the sort of people that like you not because you do something for them, but because they enjoy your company.

Being a people pleaser is a problem that takes up your entire schedule, because you will start saying "yes" to every request or favor, whether it is taking your neighbor's kid to his soccer practice, or going with a co-worker to help her find a new dress which will lead to not having enough time for you and your personal growth. After a while, you will start ignoring the signs your own body gives you. For example, if you waste the entire day doing favours for others, you won't have enough time to eat a healthy dinner, and you will grab whatever food you can find before crashing and then repeating the entire process the following day. In time, this will affect both your physical and mental health. So, the best way to deal with this is to set your goals and abide by them. Let's say that you love acting and enjoy your time on stage, but you don't find time to take classes.

My suggestion is easy - force yourself to find the time and do it. Take those classes, and set your goals in terms of months and years. Let's continue to use the acting example: set yourself a goal of taking classes on Shakespearian acting, and act in a play. This might take time, and of course, unexpected problems might arise, such as health or monetary problems, but always keep your eyes on the goal. Write down this goal, and look at it every day: "In six months I will be playing Othello at the local theatre". Whenever people try to ask you for a favor, you might feel compelled to say yes. However, if it interferes with your schedule, try to avoid doing it. Focus all your strength and mind on your goal. After a while, you will start seeing progress, and that's the best part of all. Also, your friends and the people around you will encourage you to keep doing it.

However, everything isn't that easy. Sometimes, in our group of friends or coworkers, there is someone who always asks you for a favor. They have something that needs to be done, and they can't understand that you need your own time. They might even criticize your choice of clothing, or start saying negative things about your goals. They may say things like: "You won't be able to do it". Don't let them get to you. This sort of person is what is sometimes called a Toxic Person. When you meet one of those, you feel like they want to be your friend and enjoy your company. But the reality is, when you keep getting negativity from them, the best way to deal with it is to simply avoid them. Keep them out of your life.

Another factor to keep in mind is that people pleasers are prone to manipulation, and toxic people are the best at that. They twist and change facts to make you feel bad, or they may even lie to make you out to be the villain. And then, when everybody forgot or time has passed, they will ask something from you, and you will be compelled to say yes because perhaps they won't do it again and they simply made a mistake. Well, the truth is, they didn't, and they will undoubtedly take advantage of you in ways that perhaps aren't that obvious. You need to learn how to spot them, and the most obvious hint is that they will always flatter you with phrases or statements like: "You are great at cooking, would you cook something for my family's meeting?"

This might sound like an innocent request, until you start to realize that it will not only take an entire night to do, but the family also have special needs in their foods, and you will obviously have to buy everything, prepare it, cook it (main menu and desserts), and you won't get paid at all. Like I mentioned before, you have to learn how to refuse these types of requests. If saying "no" outright is difficult for you and these sort of people will make you feel guilty for even thinking about it, then try to say "I will check on you later" or "I will get back to you". This will avoid the entire problem if you are uncomfortable with it, and then you can send an email or a text later saying that you don't have time for that sort of commitment. Always keep in mind that the best option is to deal with this upfront.

Signs of a Toxic Person and Their Behaviours

1. Comparing themselves to others

This is the universal behavior of all the toxic behaviors that toxic people share, and is one that you perhaps do without knowing that it is toxic. The desire and push to look at others and compare their lives with your own is an exercise in futility because no matter what you are comparing yourself to, you will always find faults. And the reason is obvious - nobody has the same experiences and feelings as you. Each and every experience that you had in your life shapes you and changes your future. You wouldn't compare a kid from the worst part of India to a kid born in the richest part of Switzerland, because they both have different opportunities.

Physical appearance, your wealth, parents, family, health, and even the global economic situation will shape you and a person born right next to you in a completely different way. That's where empathy comes to play; if you understand their past and their experiences, you will understand their behavior, which is something that a toxic person never does.

2. Creating Drama

You know when you are at a social gathering or in the office and someone tells you that someone in the other group thinks you have bad breath? Yeah, that's drama. Perhaps the details are different, but we always experience some kind of drama like that. And sometimes, toxic people love this, because it gives them the attention they crave as they are in the middle of the conflict, even if they are provoking it.

In offices and in your personal life, these people will never admit that what they did was wrong. They only "wanted you to know", and they will always say that they do it to protect you. Toxic people tend to do it on a daily, almost hourly basis, and you have to put an effort to quell the fire and avoid conflict. Nothing good will come from it, and you will end up emotionally drained, while the toxic person gets happy from the attention. Act calm and think cool, and if you act like this, you will quickly undermine any kind of drama that might come your way. They want you to get riled up. Don't give them the pleasure. This is your best weapon against drama.

3. Negative views

The way you speak about yourself will speak to the rest, and if you continuously make self-deprecating comments about your health, physical appearance, and opinions, people will stop taking you seriously. At the same time, if you tend to express negative views or critique others without being asked, people will take it as a sign that you cannot be trusted. After all, they will be sure that after they turn their backs, you will start saying the same thing about them.

Starting with just one or two negative comments can lead you down a spiral of negativity, especially if you get praised after such comments. Avoid them like the plague, and be aware of people who do it around you, whether they are friends or even family.

4. Seeking Validation

While spending time with people is a fantastic and beautiful experience, you shouldn't be reliant on them to make you feel worthy or happy. If any action that you take is to seek the validation of people around you, it will be impossible for you to have peace of mind. The only opinion about yourself that you should pay attention to is your own because you will never be perfect to the rest of the world. They can help give you self assurance and confidence, but your own opinion and self-view should be what guides your actions.

Toxic people will insist that you listen to them because they know what's best for you. They will always cover their true intentions (to bring you down) by acting like they want the best for you. Perhaps they do it unconsciously, but the reality is, more often than not, their tips and guides are not what's best for you and your mental health.

5. Perfectionism

Striving to become better isn't a bad idea, and, later, I will show you how the top businessmen do it every day, which is one of the secrets of their success. However, perfectionism is being obsessed with doing everything absolutely perfectly. In simple terms, it is improvement taken to the extreme.

Athletes strive for perfection, to a certain extent. There are people like Cristiano Ronaldo who arrive early to train and stay three or four hours after it finishes to continue exercising. This is a perfect way to tackle whatever problem you might have, but even people like him know that you cannot be perfect, and trying to be so is harmful to your health. Pushing yourself is fine, but doing it to an extreme is a problem that you must avoid.

In the same vein, if you are an artist or if you ever created a piece of art, you will know that after a point, you have to let it go and tackle it again in the future, or even just publish it how it is. No matter how hard you try, your book, painting or piece of music will never be perfect, and trying to make it so is a risk as you will be become obsessed with it and never finish it. Perfectionism is a toxic behavior that can ruin your life and that of those around you, because you will neglect to spend time with them and your own health will suffer. Be aware of these attitudes in your family or coworkers, because when you are under tight deadlines, you will never finish and problems will ensue. Remember - after a while of working to the best of your abilities, it is good to just let it go.

6. Taking Things Personally

This tip goes hand in hand with tip number 2. You heard that someone made comments behind your back, so you go and confront them, even if you don't have any evidence that the comment was directed at you or your loved ones. This toxic behavior is dangerous because not only can it lead to physical altercations, it can also destroy relationships just like that.

And it isn't just due to negative comments, but also when we assume that someone's annoyance, displeasure, sadness or anger is our fault and we start a thought process that is sometimes hard to get out of. We start to get paranoid and believe that everything that they do is our fault, while in reality, our actions don't always have that much impact. If you behave like this, you really need to stop thinking that it is about you, and if you have questions, practice some empathy and tactfully ask the other person if there's anything you can do to help. Toxic people, however, will never do this, and will always believe that they are the cause of all your problems. This, in turn, will create drama and of course, that's the last thing we want. If you take responsibility for things that are way under your control, your sense of self-worth will take a hit. Always remember this.

7. Living in the past

The first time that I saw Back to the Future, I remember that my greatest desire at the time was to have a time machine so I could go back and make things right. After a while, I realized that it would be really bad, not just because of temporal paradoxes (while interesting to explore, they aren't the purpose of this book), but because every act that I did or I didn't do is what shaped me to be the person that I am today.

However, some people cannot let the past die. They always talk about the "good old times", when everything was great and there weren't any problems. This toxic behavior is quite serious because they tend to ignore the problems or conflicts that existed in the past and only remember the good things. Living in the past is useless, and like all useless things, it must be discarded and ignored. This, of course, doesn't mean to never remember where you are from or your experiences, but to learn from them and not commit the same mistakes again. The past is perfect when it comes to teaching you lessons to apply in the present, but it isn't a place to stay in for more than a few minutes. Remember people fondly, and remember what they taught you.

Leave the past in the past, and enjoy the present moment.

8. Having their heads in the future

Dreaming and wishing are healthy habits, and you could use them to set a goal to fulfill and accomplish. That's the best part of being human - you can plan things.

But the reality is that the future, no matter how hard we try, cannot be predicted. If we could predict it, we would all be millionaires. Planning is one thing, but becoming obsessed with the future can lead to anxiety and worry, which are problems that are better to avoid. Keep in mind that being a bit worried is normal, but when it becomes an obsession, that's where you have to stop and control your emotions. You cannot prepare things that haven't happened yet, and while having dreams and goals are great, they have to always remain possibilities.

If you focus on the future too much, you won't enjoy the present and all the good things that it has. Enjoy the moment, and deal with the future when it comes. Remember the famous saying, "You will cross that bridge when you get to it."

9. Playing The Victim

This is a very familiar toxic behavior, and it usually comes from people who were dealt a bad hand at life. If you suffered trauma or a severe health problem, after you deal with it to the best of your abilities, you must not allow this toxic behavior to be the root of your thoughts. You have control of the present and the future, no matter what happened in the past.

My cousin got hit by a car and went blind when he was 13 years old. That, of course, left a mark on his life and his aspirations to become a filmmaker. However, after much thought, he decided that while the crash took his sight, it wouldn't take his life and his love for it. He wouldn't become a victim to negativity. He changed his outlook on life and decided that the best way is to let the past die and enjoy the present. Now, no matter what happens to our family, we can always rely on him for a good laugh. His way of thinking makes us really happy, and we are really proud that he decided to combat this toxic behavior.

10. Selfishness

This is the complete opposite of being a people pleaser, and you might fall into it if you are trying to overcompensate your behavior. This a toxic behavior that is completely detrimental to your mental welfare, because acting in a selfish and egocentric way will make the people around you distrust you and keep you at a distance. Selfishness drives people away and breaks the trust that people have in you. That trust is something that you have to cherish and treasure like gold.

Toxic people always do things for their own benefit, and they don't care what others think, or if they get hurt in the process. They are obsessed with their goals and will step over anybody that challenges them. At the same time, in their work environment, they always do everything for their own benefit. If the rest of the team cannot be saved, they believe that it's not their problem. They won't give you a hand and won't help you whenever you might have a problem. They go hand in hand with people pleasers, because they manipulate people to get the most out of that relationship and give nothing in return.

Keep an eye out for them, because they will leave you emotionally drained. They are toxic, and sadly, it is a behavior that is quite common, and sometimes even encouraged.

11. Sense of Entitlement

Some people believe that the rest of the world owes them something, be it money, attention, power, or anything else. These people are toxic, and their behavior rots them to the core, to the point that it is hard to establish a relationship with them.

Entitlement will make you believe that you are the best and that good things should happen to you no matter what you do. It will make you feel like people who don't help you are against you and are doing everything to put you down. The reality is that people don't really deserve anything, and they have to earn whatever they want or need. They have to fight for what they believe and become the change that they want to see in the world. Nobody will give them success.

Entitled people tend to believe that if they aren't succeeding, it is because the rest of the world hates them. Keep an eye out if you ever fall into this behavior, as it is a habit that is hard to break from.

12. Judging Others

Passing judgments to everybody around you is the best and safest way to make them leave you alone. Remember, you can only see from your own perspective, and you don't know what demons they are fighting every day or what problems they might have.

While you are free to watch and observe the choices and actions that others do, always be aware that you cannot fully understand the reasons for them, since there is no way to read their mind. Perhaps they don't even know why they do the things that they do, so how could you know better than them? If you pass judgment to others, especially if you aren't asked to, you are entering a toxic behavior maze that is hard to escape. When you judge someone on how they dress or talk, you project your own beliefs and experiences onto them, especially when you are saying that you would do things differently. Passing judgement like this says more about you than the person being judged.

Toxic people will always do this and will ask you to join them in their behavior because they seek confirmation and validation that what they are doing is right and that everybody does it. But never give in. Don't give them weapons that they can use to later hurt you. You are under no obligation to become like them, and you don't have to stay with them because you have other, better friends. Like a tumor, extirpate those toxic people from your life.

13. Arrogance

We are victims of arrogance, whether we like it or not. We always do this, sometimes even unconsciously. We believe that in certain situations, we are better than somebody we are comparing ourselves to. This is a toxic behavior that we must eradicate.

This is something that people encourage because, in movies, we often see arrogant characters get what they want. But in real life, an arrogant person will quickly be left alone, without friends and with quite a few problems at work because of his attitude. Arrogance always goes hand in hand with a lack of empathy and compassion, and it is a toxic behavior where the only true victim is yourself. You will be left alone, and that's exactly what we are trying to change.

If you ever think that you are better than someone and that they can't tell you anything because they don't really know you, then you are an arrogant person. Change the way you think. Change it, realize that you aren't better than anyone, and only then can you become a better person. But face your arrogance, because it's one of the obstacles between you and your happiness.

14. Being Overly Competitive

The road towards arrogance is being overly competitive. While being competitive in itself isn't bad, and is actually encouraged in team-related activities or at the office. However, when you go out of your way to compete with anyone about the smallest things, and then believing that you are better, that's when you have a problem.

It will cause problems with your family, as well as your friends. It is one of the most common toxic behaviors around, and it can be taught in the family. It is a small voice in your head that says that you have to win this competition because you fear that you won't be loved as much if you don't. The worse comes when you are validated in this behavior when people, sometimes unknowingly, encourage you to become more competitive. This creates a loop where you get more competitive, and people enjoy it, which in turn leaves you even more competitive, and so on.

Being overly competitive can create serious health-related

issues and cause problems with your self-image. Also, it may lead to becoming obsessed with perfection, which, as we said, is an addictive toxic behavior.

15. Stubbornness

Having an opinion or an idea is great. Being stubborn when it has been proved that the idea doesn't work is not. There are always stubborn people in the business world that people adore, but you still have to be open to new ideas and concepts that come up in your journey. The titans that run the industry today (Elon Musk, Jeff Bezos, etc) aren't where they are because they were set on one idea and never changed and evolved in their lives. Even Steve Jobs, a man that by all accounts was a stubborn man, knew when to adapt his ideas to the rules of the market or to the technology available at the time.

When you are in a group of friends, being stubborn will work against you most of the time, because you have to be able to negotiate and work towards a common goal. For example, let's say that all of you want to go out to eat, and you are absolutely stuck on the idea of getting sushi, even though nobody in the group likes it. They decide that they would like some pizza, and you end up angry at them because they didn't listen to you. The night is then ruined for both you and your friends.

A stubborn person falls into this behavior because they

believe that they know better than the rest, and it is often arrogance that makes them act the way they are. Be aware of this behavior so you can change your opinions and adapt accordingly to your environment. However, this does not mean that you should lose your values and forget your ideas and opinions just because the rest of the world doesn't like them. Strike a balance between the extremes. To do this, the best way is to practice your negotiation abilities. Tonight we will all eat pizza, but next week, you can order sushi or whatever you want. That's the truth behind the success of Bezos, Musk and other successful people - they know how to negotiate. Become one of them by practicing and mastering this skill.

16. Ignoring Self-care

Under no situation must you ignore your own health. Toxic people will encourage you to do it, saying that "doctors don't really know" and that they know best because a cousin or a friend had whatever you have and got better without really doing anything.

This is absolutely wrong and incredibly dangerous. Here, I'm not just talking about your physical health, but also your mental health. Ignoring the signs of burnout or being under a tremendous amount of stress can lead to several problems in the short and long- term. There is no shame to go to a doctor when you feel bad, or to a therapist whenever you feel like something is missing in your life. Perhaps therapy can help you tackle problems that you didn't know you had.

In my personal experience, going to a therapist is one of the best things that I ever did because he gave me the tools to create and maintain my mental fortitude, even when I'm struggling with depression and anxiety. Go to therapy, ask them for a session (some of them even offer the first one for free) and see if you can talk about what is going on your mind. Most of the time, we start talking and suddenly realize that we have been talking for three hours and find out that we have more problems than we imagined. Try it.

17. Not Speaking Out

Not all toxic behavior involves actions. Sometimes, toxic behavior happens when you don't raise your hand when you should, before any damage is done. If you see that you can't reach a deadline and accept another job, you may risk failing both your client and yourself. Raising your hand and admitting that you may be able to reach a deadline is the best way to face it, before the problem explodes in your face, with consequences (sometimes monetary) for everybody involved.

In the same vein, whenever you see a wrong attitude and don't speak out, you are risking not just your health, but also that of those around you. If you don't say "look, I believe this is wrong and you should stop", you may become an accomplice in that bad behavior. Toxic people will always stay silent, because they want drama, or perhaps they want to avoid conflict. Then, they will wash their hands and say that they didn't do it. They are very rarely held accountable for not speaking out, and they get away with it.

If you notice bad behavior, speak out, from the smallest to more important things. Speak out, and then face it knowing that you did the right thing not remaining silent.

18. Holding On To Loss

I previously mentioned how dangerous it is to have our mind in the past, and how addictive it can be. The same can be said about losses. Life is what it is because we have the good along with the bad, and sometimes, the bad is losing someone that we love.

For example, I still miss Rocks and I wish that he was still with me. We would still have adventures, and he would play with my son. I would give him his favorite food every night because he surely deserves it. But the truth is that he's gone, and he's not coming back. While the spiritual side of death is not something that I'm great at, I always faced loss by feeling like it was a new start. After Rocks passed away, I met John, and while some part of me is inclined to believe that wherever Rocks was, he was helping me somehow, the truth is that if I wasn't depressed, I wouldn't have met him, and then set down the path that I'm on right now. My wife once told me a great quote from Star Wars:

"Death is a natural part of life. Rejoice for those around you who transform into the Force. Mourn them do not. Miss them do not. Attachment leads to jealousy. The shadow of greed, that is."

I love this quote because it basically means that staying attached to one thing will lead to jealousy, which is another toxic behavior. Although they are talking about how the Jedis cannot have material possessions or attachments, I believe that it is a quote that we can apply to everyday life.

Let go, and learn from your losses. If you lost your job or your independence, learn from it, and use this as a new start to become a better version of yourself. If we work hard enough, life has a way of opening new doors. In time, it will happen to you too.

19. Insincerity

Be true to your own self. That's the best advice that I can ever give you. Be true to your values, to what you hold dear, and to your opinions. Perhaps they will change when you also change, but never change your own personality to become what is expected from you.

Show people around you your true personality, and interact with them. Show them the great person that you are (because I'm sure you are). You might be inclined to think that if you were another person you would have greater success in life or at work, but after a while, it will be impossible to keep lying to yourself, and you will start questioning who you really are.

Toxic people will always say that you should change and become like them because they are successful and you are not. They say that you should imitate them, copy their behavior, and follow their lead. That's absolutely toxic, and you have to avoid this at all cost. A suggestion is fine, but when they push you to become like them, you will realize that they are a toxic person. Don't listen to them. Listen to your own self.

20. Cruelty

Whenever you feel insecure or under pressure, it is easy to fall prey to this behaviour. You think that perhaps no one will notice a little cruelty here and there. But while small slip-ups are understandable, when you start relying on being a bad person or just insulting others to feel better about yourself, it is incredibly detrimental to your life and to the life of those around you.

People don't want cruel people around them, and they avoid them at all costs. The cost of being cruel is isolation. If you see someone being cruel to another person, speak up and don't stay silent. People will remember your attitudes and actions during these situations, and however you react, always do it with your conscience and your heart.

21. Attention Seeking

Being a people pleaser is basically looking for attention in the form of validation because we offer ourselves to anybody who needs help. Seeking attention from others is an addictive behavior, and it has a great impact on your health in the long-term.

If you see that people love you because you are always backing them up and doing things for them, try to distance yourself from that group. That way, you will see if they really liked you, or they just loved the things that you did for them and how you made them feel.

22. Jealousy

Jealousy is a cancer that will rot every relationship that you have. At work, this toxic behaviour will always make you see what other people do, and will make you wish that you were like them. You will end up criticizing them, and that will lead to the rest of the toxic behaviours that we mentioned in this list.

Jealousy is also a way to distance yourself from everyone

around you because you tend to resent others for gaining or doing the same thing that you do, to the point that you may end up alone due to this behavior.

23. Resisting New Experiences

I mentioned that to become an interesting person, you have to experience new things and eat food that you've never eaten before. However, worrying about the future will make you resist these new experiences. You will lie in your comfort zone, avoid any risks or problems, and then wonder why you aren't attractive to the rest of the world.

Going outside and experimenting will help you to get the best out of your life. Don't avoid new things in favour of the known, even when you know that doing what you already know is the best way to live a safe life. Don't live a safe life, go out and take a risk. We only live once, and we have to make the most of it.

24. Lying

All relationships, no matter what kind, are based and built on mutual trust. This is quite easy to break, especially when there are lies involved. We believe what our friend tells us and accept it as the truth.

But when we find out our friend lied to us, the trust that we had in them evaporates like water on a hot day, and from that moment on, you won't be able to look at them the same way. While honesty is not easy, it is important to your own health and happiness and to those of the people involved. If you keep a lie, you will never find lasting peace, especially if you deny your true self.

Chapter 4

How to Make New Friends

(and not die in the process)

If you've ever seen little kids playing at recess, you will have noticed that kids don't care about *how* they make new friends. They just walk up to another kid, ask if they can play together, and that's it! That friendship might last twenty minutes or an entire lifetime, but it doesn't matter. What matters is that they share a common passion (for example, dinosaurs, or superheroes), and want to share it with someone else and have fun.

But for adults, this is extremely hard. You can't walk up to someone and ask if they want to play with trucks (well, you *can*, and I will teach you how to do it without sounding weird). When you are an adult, you keep thinking that it might sound bad to share something like that, or that the rest will think that you are childish. Or even worse, we are afraid of being rejected, so we avoid those kind of situations. This is a vicious cycle because if we don't put ourselves out there, we won't make new friends. If we don't make new friends, we will start having problems with our social skills. And if we do have friends, we always have other responsibilities, like family or work, and that doesn't leave us with enough time to hang out with them. When we are kids, we have all the time in the world, because our number one priority is to have play and have fun. But as grownups, fun and games have almost no place in our lives.

In previous chapters, I spoke about how important it is to dedicate enough time for your wellbeing, and now you will start seeing exactly why this is important. Remember the example that I mentioned about kids sharing a passion or a love for something? Well, that's what organizations or clubs are for. Passionate people love to share their love for something to the rest of the world.

In my city, there is a small group of stamp collectors that get together once a month at a local café to share stories and stamps. At first glance, you might be inclined to think that it is a moot point, but the truth is that they share such a passion for something as simple as a stamp (or at least, I thought it was simple until I got there and talked to them). They have been doing it for the past ten years at least, and during that time, friendships were created, to the point of almost becoming like family. It is a passion that passes through generations. They enjoy a good coffee and talk for almost six or seven hours. After a while, they share stamps and talk about places to get your hands on some that are particularly hard to get or special offers that you can find online.

As a kid, I didn't have much interest in stamps, but after

talking to them for an entire afternoon, I was compelled to go out and buy something. I ended up not getting any stamps (my love for collecting goes against my love for living without any extra stuff), but I did make some new, great friends. We realized that we share a passion for food and wine, and we decided to create a group specialized in those two things so we can meet other people like us. It might sound strange to some of you, but the truth is that there are many people out there who share the same love for an activity and want to meet people like them. Try to search in your city (Google and Facebook are great for that) to see if you can find a group that shares your interests. Chances are that there might already be a couple. If you find any that suits your tastes, ask them if you can go to their next meeting. They will surely welcome you with open arms.

If there isn't a group already created, you can find out the place to host one. For example, something small like a stamp collection or a book club is best hosted in a quiet coffee shop. On the other hand, for something like acting or cosplaying (getting dressed up as a video game or movie character), you will probably need a bigger space. Talk to the owners and ask them how much it costs to rent the place, or if they will allow you to meet with your group. Most times, the owners will allow it only if your group orders something to eat or drink. Post it on social media, like on your city's Facebook group, and then organize how to do it with the other interested people.

Perhaps they might even have better ideas.

Another suggestion would be to take classes on something that you want to learn. Have you always wanted to play the guitar and compose your very own romantic ballads? This is the perfect time to do it. Find out if there's any guitar teacher close to you. While this idea might be more expensive (after all, you will need a guitar), you will know for sure that the people in those classes will share a love for the instrument, so you will at least know that you can talk to them about that.

Group related activities are great for people who want to make new friends. If you are a sports fan, then your best chances are to go to a club and ask if you can join them. When it comes to sports, you might feel like you have to be Messi or Cristiano Ronaldo to be accepted, and while some teams might be competitive, there are several teams that enjoy playing together simply for fun. The best way to approach it is to have a laid back and relaxed attitude. If you spend time with your team at practices or games, you will see that it is an easy way to get close to others, and like the guitar lesson example, you share the same passion. In these types of situations, approaching or talking to people isn't as hard as you might think, and you already know how to do it:

Talk to them like you were a kid with a truck and were in search of a buddy.

Yes, when you are in group activities, it is that simple. For example, let's say that you love football, and are a fan of a particular team. At one point, during the break, you see that there are a small group of players talking about the last Barcelona match. But wait, you saw that one! You love that team. You know what you have to do in that case, and it is quite simple. Go to them, listen to what they are saying, and try to talk about how great Messi is, or how that last play deserved a red card. Try not to overwhelm them with your opinion, because they need to be heard too. Just approach the conversation, first by listening, and then when you see a cue, ask a question about the match, even if you already know the answer. This will make your interlocutor listen to you. Be assertive and secure. With this, you will see that they will start paying attention to you and your opinions. Listen to them, look at them in the eyes when they are talking, and wait for your turn to speak.

When you are in a conversation with someone you don't know, you are aware of every move they make and look for signs displaying any sort of emotion. In the same vein, the other person in the conversation is looking for the same symptoms in how you act. This might sound weird, but we do it all the time, sometimes even unconsciously. Perhaps it is something ingrained in our brains or genes, but the fact is that we tend to listen and pay attention to someone who smiles and express confidence. Have you ever been to a critical business meeting? In those, you will see that everybody in that meeting has a perfect posture (especially when it comes to CEOs), speak clearly and concisely, and don't hesitate at all when making decisions.

One thing that you have to keep in mind is that your body language is everything. If you straighten your back, have a firm voice and look people in the eyes when you are talking, everybody will take you seriously. Let me give you an example so you can see exactly what I'm talking about:

Let's say that you have to give a business presentation for your bosses and the company CEO. This presentation is critical, and the future of the company depends on this meeting. The CEO doesn't have time for small talk, as she's a very busy woman, so you can't start by talking about your life or saying a joke. You enter the conference office, and you see that five people are sitting around the conference table waiting for your talk.

This could go two ways. If you go unsure of what you have to say and start stumbling on your words, the presentation is over, and it is a failure. Your future at the company might be compromised, or at least, your performance report at the end of the year will take a hit. This, in turn, will lead to a lower salary increase, and obvious problems will follow.

But if you enter the room like you own it, look everyone in the eyes, and have a loud voice (this doesn't mean shouting, of course), no matter what you are saying, and even if perhaps you don't have all the necessary information, people in that meeting will still take you seriously and listen to every word you are saying. Researchers have found that one of the best ways to address a room is to learn everybody's name, their job position, and to make eye contact with all of them. People tend to pay more attention if you refer to them by name, except when it comes to senior agents. Be concise, direct, and firm. This is the basis of every expert that you might have seen on the internet.

When it comes to having a conversation with someone that you don't know, experts recommend something different than what we have spoken about above. The best way to approach a discussion is to listen to every word they say, and repeat them in your own mind. This way, you are making sure that you understand every single word they say. They might be talking about something mundane, but always keep in mind that to them, it might be important. Never underestimate the importance of any subject that you're spoken to about. They might be talking about a movie they saw, but perhaps for them, that movie means much more than they can express. With experience, I learned that the key is to understand your interlocutor. Listen, comprehend, and be ready to ask direct questions. Let's use the movie example:

"What actors are in it?"

"Who is the director?"

"Does it have a good script?"

These questions might be familiar and obvious, but they are essential in showing that you listen to the other side of the conversation. Let's say that they are talking about a World War II drama, and Steven Spielberg worked on it. In this hypothetical example, you can suggest other movies from the same director. If they like the World War II theme, you can always recommend them some other classic films set in that period. Or perhaps you haven't seen any, but you know the main actors. In that case, recommend movies with the same protagonist.

But let's say that you don't know movies that well, or never cared about actors or directors. In this case, if you want to create a friendship with your interlocutor, ask them to recommend some movies. People love talking about their passion or the things that they love. If they tell you to watch a particular video or show interest in a film that is currently playing in theatres, ask them if they want to go see it with you. Doing this, you will show interest in what other people like, and also, propose a plan to do something together. If they say no, don't take it personally. Perhaps they don't know you that well yet, or maybe they have plans that day. No matter the answer, never get angry. There will be another chance.

But, you might be thinking, what about when that person refuses your invitations several times? The answer can be a little painful, but it is the sort of answer that we will find ourselves dealing with sometime during our lives. The answer is that that person might not like us, or at least, not to the extent of going out with us. This is normal, and this doesn't mean that we are at fault. More often than not, people don't like each other. Perhaps there is something in their previous experiences that makes them afraid of creating or establishing new relationships, or maybe the answer lies somewhere that we can never really know. Always remember that there is nothing wrong with you or your personality.

Best tips to have a conversation

1   Make small talk.

Sociologists have a rule that indicates that the best way to create a fluid conversation is to keep one important rule in mind: 30% talking and 70% listening. This is a general rule, and obviously, it will change from situation to situation, so keep that in mind. But in general terms, this will make you an interesting person to talk to, because you will pay attention and ask correct and specific questions. This, in due time, will make you a desirable person to talk to.

2   At the end of a conversation, don't forget to introduce yourself

This is only applicable if it is a first-time conversation, but it is a great way to ensure that the other person knows and remembers your name. Try to say something like "By the way, I'm…" More often than not, the other person will do the same. Always remember names, because that is a great way to make impressions on people. You will be more inclined to talk to someone who remembered your name or anything else that you told them. Also, if you remember their name, you will not only look smart and intelligent, but they will see that you were paying attention.

3   Ask them out for coffee

We talked about this tip before, but it is important to expand on this. A social gathering gives you a better opportunity to truly know another person, in a way that perhaps might not be possible in another context. Invite them to get some coffee or to go to the theater. To organize and plan with them, you can give them your phone number or email address. This gives them the possibility to contact you at any time. Don't worry if they don't give you their information in return, because that's fine. There will be time for that in the future, once you get to know each other. One handy way to extend your invitation is to say something along the lines of "I gotta go, but what about we go out some time, maybe to get coffee or for lunch? Here's my phone number if you ever want to call me." Perhaps they don't have enough time to make new friends. I mentioned this before - don't take it personally. Offer your contact information to people who have the potential to be a good friend, and in time, somebody will get back to you.

These steps are clear, direct, and simple. But like every step that we talked about in this book, while this might help, it doesn't replace professional help. If you feel like you can't implement these steps, and no matter what you do, you can't make new friends, then the best solution is to seek professional help. Going to a shrink isn't a big deal, and there is absolutely no shame in it. Do what you can to get better, and the first step to do it is to deal with it.

Chapter 5

Dull Conversations

Congratulations, the guy you talked to called to see if that invitation for coffee was still on. You have a new friend! So you both decide on a date, place, and activity. The appointment comes, you sit down to talk and get to know each other, and then you notice that the conversation dies as soon as one of you stops talking. No matter how hard you both try, ultimately, the conversation dies. Even if you go back to your main passion (the one you talked about the first time), the dullness and repetitiveness bore you both. After a while, one of you decides to call it a night and go home. You go home confused. What happened? Everything seemed to be going great the first time, what happened the second time?

Dull conversations are the main obstacle that you will face when you try to form a new relationship with anybody. It is something that you have to actively fight in every conversation, and if it is left unchecked, it will poison the bond that you have with that particular person. But the way to confront this is quite easy, and if you practice every day, you will become an expert at handling this.

In my experience, the best way to engage and create a fun environment for conversations is to find out what turns people on. No, I do not mean it that way, I'm talking about being turned on emotionally. This is the first step that you have to take, and at the same time the hardest, because you will be blind in this. The idea behind this step of the conversation is to find out what stimulates the other person on an emotional level, and as the name suggests, it might get emotional. Never talk about heavy subjects, at least in the first few times. If the other person needs to talk about a certain heavy subject, the subject will come up naturally. You can use this heavy subject list as a guide to see what is best to avoid:

-    Abortion and health-related topics

-    Religion (this is quite an important one, particularly because many people see religion as a way of life, so, unless you both share the same religion, try to avoid this one at all cost)

-    Politics

-    In some cases: Sports

While the rest might be quite obvious, you might be thinking that sports shouldn't be on that list, but the truth is that many people take sports way too seriously and will defend their colours or team with a passion. Unless you are knowledgeable on the subject, it's best to stay away from this topic.

Other subjects might be off the table depending on the case (for example, if you see that your interlocutor has a disability, don't bring that up unless the subject comes up naturally), but in general terms, the list should help you stay clear of any problems. With that being said, if your values are rooted in those subjects (you might have a firm opinion on abortion or current politics), always be aware that while people might have an opinion on it, it does not mean that they necessarily want to share it.

We talked about finding out what the other person loves. One quick way to break the social rule or norm that might rule over the conversation (like small talk) is to stop using social scripts or if possible, avoid asking questions that society makes us feel like we need to ask. To do this, go out of your way to learn about that person's life:

- "What has been the best part of your year?"

- "What do you as a hobby?"

- "Leaving work aside, what is your main objective during the day?"

Let me tell you a story. A close friend of mine met her life partner at a party. My friend was drinking quietly when her future wife approached her and asked her about her t-shirt. She was wearing a Seven Samurai t-shirt (a classic Japanese movie by Akira Kurosawa) and, at first, was surprised to find other people that knew the movie. But then, the talk went from old classic movies to other topics, never falling in the same "do you come here often?" or "what's your zodiac sign?" routine. This kept the conversation interesting, and when she had to go, she asked her if she wanted to go to watch a movie together the following week. They exchanged numbers and found out that they had a lot in common, aside from just movies. They have been married for the past seven years, and it fills me with joy every time they bring up the story of how they met.

While this story ended up with both people married to each other (and profoundly and thoroughly in love, if I may add), this doesn't mean that every relationship you have in your life will have a romantic outcome. Perhaps you find your wife or husband, or maybe you find a true friend, but the important thing is that you will get someone that you can trust and talk to. This is one of the most important things that you can get in your life, so treasure it deeply.

According to several researchers on the topic, what guides our relationships and our interaction with the rest of the world is to feel important, to feel cherished, and to find other interesting people. This is normal, and this does not mean that we are all selfish (although if you need this a bit too much, you may end up having an egocentric personality, so be careful). The psychology behind this is quite straightforward: if you can make someone feel unique and special by listening and paying attention to their opinions, feelings or ideas, you will in turn become attractive to them.

When you talk to someone and want to show them your appreciation, you can try to ask them questions to find out what they believe to be significant (using the guide I posted above). When they give you an answer, you can push their ideas a little further. This is tricky: Let's say that you ask them about what they love the most in the world. Their answer is "Carpentry". In this particular case, you could ask them why and how that thing or action (Carpentry) is important for them. But this does not mean that you can push them around. Don't go hard on them. Remember, you are trying to be interesting, so avoid being aggressive.

If you are talking to someone at a party, try to commit to them entirely. Don't stay on your phone or talk to anyone other than the person you are talking to at that moment. If you dedicate your entire attention to that specific person, they will feel important and worthy of attention and do their best to earn it. Smile if it is a good story, laugh if it is funny, or show sadness if it is a sad story. Don't take a trip to the bathroom so you can check emails or upload a picture to the internet. People will eventually realize this and may stop talking to you. After all, their time is important, so why would they bother with someone who doesn't value it?

Your posture is also a window into your interest in the

other person. People unconsciously pick up body signs that show us that people pay attention to them, or that they are ignoring them. Other than avoiding to check your phone, the following are several tips that you might not know about:

The direction of your toes. Yes, it sounds quite silly, but as I said, this is one of those signs that we pick up without even knowing. If you keep your toes pointed to the person speaking, their brains will pick up your feet direction and use that sign to gauge interest. If you are listening to someone talk about their experiences as a father, you can make them feel valued and worthy of your attention by keeping your torso and toes pointed at them while they speak. It's a non-verbal way to express interest and say "go on, I'm listening".

The **triple nod** is a way of expressing interest. It might sound weird at first, but studies have proved that people tend to speak two to four times longer if you give them a triple nod. This works as a subconscious cue to keep going and expand their story. When someone finishes talking, and you feel that there might be more in it, look at them in their eyes and nod three times. More times than not, they will continue their story, and if they don't, you can always ask another question related to what they have been talking about.

If you see that the conversation is dying, **ask open-ended questions**. This will help to keep the conversation alive. For example, let's say that your interlocutor is talking about old Roman History, and you see that the discussion is reaching a phase where both of you don't know what to say. In that case, ask something that might take a while to fully answer. In the example that we were talking about, ask about the differences between Romans and Greeks, and how each civilization adapted to the other. Keep in mind that I'm just giving random examples based on conversations that I had in the past, and you can always ask whatever you want. This will help to avoid "yes" and "no" answers, allow your interlocutor to express himself, and share more information that you can use to continue the conversation.

Perhaps this is the perfect time to mention it, but conversations shouldn't be like a police interrogation. While a bit of questioning is fine, it can't be at the expense of your interlocutor's peace. I suggested furthering the conversation a bit more, but never push it to the point that you make the other person feel uncomfortable. If they don't want to answer a question, or they wish to go somewhere else to talk or do something else, let them be. They don't owe you an answer, and if they don't want to speak, they are under no obligation to do so. During my times reading and watching people interact, I've seen several awkward people forcing their views and their opinions over the rest because they wrongly believed that the primary goal of any conversation is to win the argument. This is an absolute mistake and one you should avoid at all costs.

Other things that you can use to start and keep a conversation alive is to talk about something special that they are wearing or something particular about the environment you are both in. In the story that I told you before, my friend's wife asked her about the t-shirt. This is a perfect way to start a conversation because if they are wearing a unique piece of clothing, they will be more inclined to talk about it. Or if they have another unique piece of clothing, like special earrings, for example, it can spark a conversation about where they got them and if they got them during a trip overseas. However, if they don't have anything in particular, you can always comment on your environment, and use it as a cue to talk about anything that comes to your mind. Say that at the party that you are both in, there are distinctive candles lighting up the place. In that case, you can comment that they remind you of the candles that your grandmother used to use (or whatever it tells you; of course, you do not have to follow precisely what I write here!). This, in turn, will create a snowball effect in the conversation and keep the ball rolling.

Keep practicing these steps, and with enough practice, you will see that in every conversation that you have, you will end up going far more in-depth than you expected.

But let's go down the negative road: No matter what you try, the conversation dies (or in the words of Doctor Leonard McCoy: "It's dead, Jim"). You did everything you could, and you have to understand that you are under no obligation to like every single person you meet in your life. You may create a lasting relationship with some of them, and the rest will come and go from your life. That is okay, and the best solution in these cases is to retreat and move over to another person who you might feel more connected to or have more things in common with.

Chapter 6

Conversational Cues

Okay, everything seems to be going great. You are talking, people seem interested in you and your opinions, and the conversation is alive. They laugh at your jokes and comments, and they always keep in touch with you whenever there is a party coming up or any kind of social gathering that you might enjoy. That's great! So you decide to take the very same steps with another new group, and suddenly, it doesn't work. People feel a bit overwhelmed by your presence, or they don't pay attention like the first group did. What happened? You did exactly what you did before, and they responded differently. Where did you go wrong?

Well, the obvious answer is that you probably didn't do anything wrong. People respond differently to the same stimulation (that's the best part of society), and we must adapt accordingly. We talked about how we don't act the same way in front of our bosses as we do in front of our families, and we adapt our attitude and approach of talking in an unconscious way. However, sometimes, we do things or act in ways that people who don't know us may not like. The best way to see if you are doing something that might be interpreted as an offence is to follow this guide.

Signs and conversational cues

1   Personal Space

Have you ever been in a conversation where one of the people involved is way too close to the other, almost like they were over them? This is what invasion of personal space looks like. If you are standing too close to someone, people won't care about what you are saying, because it is an intimidation tactic that is often used to overpower someone, since you are using your entire body to express your idea. This is entirely wrong, and it is something that should be avoided at all costs. In the same vein, if you are standing too far, your interlocutor won't be able to hear you correctly or give you the attention you deserve.

The best way to tackle this is to try to maintain a distance of three or four feet, and this depends on how familiar you are with that person. If it is a first-time conversation, use the range that I mentioned. But if you are quite familiar with that person, or you have seen each other before, you can talk closer. Be aware of hugs and kisses on the cheeks. People from South America and parts of Europe are used to it, and if you don't like it or are not prepared, it can result in an awkward situation. If you are hugged and don't particularly like it, you can try to politely refuse and explain that you don't enjoy it. The person should understand that hugs and invasion of

88

personal space aren't for everybody. Keep this in mind if you ever travel to South America or Spain.

2   Tone of voice

If you work in an office where there are hundreds of employees, you will encounter this problem at least twice a week. Some people don't listen to their voice to see if it is too loud. I met someone who grew up in a house where the custom was to speak loud, and this led to several problems when it was time to enter the real world, to the point that he had to go to speech therapy to see if there was any way to improve with this. While this particular case is a bit on the extreme side, you will see this happening every day. But what if you do it without even knowing?

If you are in doubt about your voice, try to record it saying anything; for example, read a paragraph from the book you are currently reading, and listen to it. Does it sound loud? If you are still in doubt, you can try to consult with a doctor. They will guide you and help you if you have any speech impediment or complication.

In a conversation, always pay attention not only to what your speaker is saying, but *how and why they are speaking*. These are as important as the message itself, and you can learn a lot about the message by watching the tone, inflexion, pitch, volume and articulation of their speech. The last thing that you want as a speaker (especially in a business setting like we mentioned before) is to have listeners misinterpret your message because you raised your voice a little, or moved your hands in an aggressive way, as this will lead to confusion.

3   Vocal Register

As a corollary to the previous point, no matter how important the message is, the tone and vocal register are what people will remember from your speech. The most important thing in a conversation is to use the correct vocal register for the topic you are discussing. For example, if it is a happy situation or a friendly gathering, you don't want to use a lower voice because that expresses sadness. Try to use a higher register in your voice to express your happiness. In the same vein, if you are at a funeral or at a hospital, you want to use a lower register because that is what is suited to the place and situation.

4   Tone of your Text

This is something that you will have to learn the hard way. No matter how much you practice, you will eventually make a mistake. But the best way to check if you are doing it correctly is to read a message you have composed on email or text two or three times after you have composed it. Sometimes, you will realize that perhaps it wasn't the best way to express yourself, and you can change or adapt accordingly. For example, if you are writing an email to your boss using your company's address, always be formal and avoid every attempt at friendship. Keep it professional, and it will be appreciated. If, however, you have a bond with your boss, then you can talk to him in a friendly manner over texts or on the phone. Be professional in a work environment, and helpful outside of it. This way, you keep a safe distance between your work life and personal life.

If you are in doubt about the tone, try to read it for a friend, family, or someone you trust. This way, they can give you an outside perspective of the situation. If they offer a critique or ideas, be open to listening to them. That's why you are talking to them, after all.

5   Fidgeting

This is a social cue that we have ingrained thanks to Hollywood and TV shows. You know when someone is playing with their hair while they are listening to you? How many times have we seen people in movies flirting with this exact move?

No matter what pop culture says, the truth is that most people take it as a universal sign of discomfort. If you are talking to someone, like a new friend, for example, and they start playing with their hair or shifting their weight from one foot to the other, they might be uninterested in the conversation or might be feeling uneasy about the subject that you are talking about. In the same vein, if you want to express and show how confident you are, you have to be aware of your fidgeting, and try your best to cut that habit out. Fidgeting is also a way to express nervousness, and you don't want that. Of course, if you are feeling uncomfortable about the subject, you can always politely tell your interlocutor that you can change the topic. Or, if you dont feel comfortable saying it, you can always just change the conversation.

6   Wardrobe choices

My mother once told me that I should "dress for the job that I want, not for the one that I have". This is a great piece of advice because it works on many levels. Unconsciously, we are more prone to following and listening to the advice of someone who is well dressed than the one of someone who doesn't care about their appearance.

On the other hand, a great way to see if your coworker or someone close to you is having a really bad time is to check their clothes. If you see that they are untidy, aren't clean, or look like a truck went over them (metaphorically speaking), you can try to talk to them to see if there's something wrong. Perhaps they are waiting for someone to ask them, and that person could be you. Practice empathy and active listening, and keep your eyes and ears open for any sign of a problem. Sometimes, our body language says more than what we actually say with words.

Chapter 7

The Secrets of Successful

People

Every time that we see a movie star on an interview or a successful person on TV, we see that they have what most of us don't, likeability. People love and admire them, and all wish they could be their friends. We want to be like them, but where can we start?

Sadly, there isn't an easy way to be successful. People are loved and liked for different things, and there isn't a catch-all answer that you can apply to every situation. However, there are steps that you can take to be successful and create a better version of yourself.

Being better is a work in progress. You have to understand that practicing every day is what made them the people that we admire today. Whether we are talking about George Clooney or Jeff Bezos, you can bet that they share many habits, and while the details might be different depending on their business, they all follow the same basis.

1   Always set a goal

What is your goal? What is your passion? What do you love, and why? These questions should be your first step. What do you want to be? Do you want to be an actor? A successful businessman? Or perhaps you want to be a politician so you can fight for the greater good?

Your answers should be yours. Write them down. Write down an essay on why you want to be that sort of person, and how are you going to do it. Put them where you can see it every day, like on a board in clear view, for example. Set down your goals and ask yourself how you are going to achieve them. If you want to become a movie star, you will have to start with the basics - acting classes. If you want to be an innovator like Steve Jobs, start by studying and reading everything you can about the subject that you love. Always push yourself a little more, and never settle for mediocrity.

When you take classes on whatever you want to study, don't just leave it at that. If acting is what you want to do, watch videos on YouTube, read books about it, go to castings, get a camera, and record yourself doing a soliloquist. It doesn't matter if it is horrible because you have to understand that your current talent will always be worse than your talent tomorrow. Always strive to be better, and you are under no obligation to be the same person that you were the day before.

2   Be Proactive

You have your goal set, and you have decided the best

way to reach it, so you decide to start tomorrow. However, you wake up that day and leave all your work for the next day. And so on and so forth for an entire month. If you are looking for success to come out of nowhere, the chances of that happening are even smaller than getting hit by an airplane while sharks are raining from the sky. Joking aside, success only comes to people who look for it. It doesn't have to be right away, and it will take time and effort. That's the hard part and the one where most people quit and decide that success isn't for them. You will have to make sacrifices, and you will have to push you and your team (if you have one) to the point of no return.

When you are learning how to do a certain task, don't just stay stuck on one idea. Go out and learn everything you can. Take notes of every book you read and every movie you see. Inspiration will come from places that you do not yet understand. For example, I once wrote a short story about a pigeon and its desire to become a human, since it saw that we could do things that were amazing from its point of view. The inspiration behind that wasn't from a pigeon but actually came from reading an old sci-fi story about a ghost who wanted to have legs again. Why did it become a pigeon in my story? I don't know, but the truth is that inspiration will come in ways that aren't clear.

Remember - successful people improve their lives by making the most of their day. Unsuccessful people only react to whatever life throws at them. They can't be bothered to understand what they have to do in order to improve themselves. Don't be that kind of person. You can be better. You have to be better. You will be better.

3   Exercise

Have you noticed that no matter what field they are in, successful people always pay attention to their health and diet? They aren't overweight, they are fit, and they look their best. Whenever we see one of those titans sick or under huge distress, we are surprised. While it is true that up to a certain point, they can control their image and what is published online, they can't control everything, no matter how hard they try.

They pay attention to their diet and spend hundreds of dollars to eat the best food available. Of course, we cannot be expected to do it right as we set our goal to be the best version of ourselves, but we can change our habits. How many times do you eat at McDonald's a week? How about you cut it down a little? Eating healthy isn't that expensive, no matter what you might be thinking. While I believe that becoming a vegetarian is the best solution for both our body and the planet, not everyone can do it because they have different health situations. Before starting to exercise or changing diets, always talk to your doctor, as they will recommend you small steps to do it.

If your doctor allows you to exercise, my personal recommendation is to get a gym membership. But if money is tight, you can go out for a run around the park. Try to do some exercise at home three times a week. Don't leave it for tomorrow. Tomorrow is now, and you have to work out.

Once you have a routine, try to adapt your life to it. If you decide to work out in the morning, wake up earlier to do so, and set your time accordingly. However, no matter how good your routine is, it will fail if you are not consistent. If you set a goal, do it. Don't make excuses or blame others, and practice will make you perfect. It will be hard, but every successful person in the world has invested hundreds of hours creating and shaping their body and soul.

4   Take responsibility not just for your success but
       also for your failures

The titans of the industry have one thing in common - they learned from their mistakes. It doesn't matter if someone else was at fault when it comes to a mistake, they had their share of responsibility, and they own it. Learn from your mistakes, because only in mistakes do we see our true self. We cannot strive to greatness and become fantastic people if we always succeed.

Failure puts us against the ropes, and it will do everything in its power to knock us down. Personally, I am a huge Rocky Balboa fan, and I always remember this line from Rocky Balboa (also known as Rocky VI):

"Let me tell you something you already know. The world ain't all sunshine and rainbows. It's a very mean and nasty place and I don't care how tough you are it will beat you to your knees and keep you there permanently if you let it. You, me, or nobody is gonna hit as hard as life. But it ain't about how hard ya hit. It's about how hard you can get hit and keep moving forward. How much you can take and keep moving forward. That's how winning is done!"

Yes, it is a Hollywood movie, and in the end, Rocky is trying to teach us something with his fist, but if you look past the character and the particular situation that the quote mentions, you can see the wisdom behind it. No matter how hard we can hit, life will hit us harder. Moreover, the best way to challenge it is to admit that we made a mistake and learn from it.

Learn from your mistake, admit that you made it, and people will take you seriously. On the other hand, if you point fingers and blame others, people will think that you are immature. When you see someone that always puts the blame on others, you start to believe that they cannot be trusted because in the future, when something goes wrong, that person may betray you and blame you for all the mistakes. Keep in mind that you are the only person that can be responsible for your own success.

5   Be Punctual

No matter if we are talking about a job interview, or a

meeting to eat something with your friend, punctuality is a skill that will greatly improve your life. Time is the only thing that we cannot gain. Once time is wasted, it cannot be earned, so you must make the most of it.

Be aware that, as precious as time is for you, the same can be said for your friends or business partners. They cherish their time, just like you, so don't leave them waiting for your presence. Always arrive fifteen minutes earlier to any meeting. If they make you wait, listen to their excuses. It is normal not to arrive on time once or twice. However, if your friend always has an excuse, then perhaps the best thing to do is to tell them how much it bothers you. Remember what we talked about earlier? Always express your problems and conflicts, but do so politely. If you do not do this, people will believe that you will wait for them no matter how late they are.

When it comes to your work and business-related deals, always be aware of your deadline. Don't ever leave whatever project you have to do to the last minute. Prepare it with enough time, and divide your tasks in smaller chunks to see if you can tackle them faster. Delegate important tasks to people you trust. Your customer pays for your time, so you don't want to let them down. Of course, sometimes life can get in the way; for example, while I was writing an article, my father got very sick, and I had to delay my delivery to focus on my father. Luckily, the client understood and gave me enough time to do both things. At the end of the day, my father got better, my client was satisfied that I was honest, and all went well.

6   Control your emotions

We mentioned this in another section of the book, but it doesn't hurt to repeat it: you cannot, under absolutely no circumstance, allow your emotions to get the best of you. No matter what happens, you have to calm down and keep them under control. Sure, you may feel like shouting, but if you want to be successful and a great leader, your emotions will get in the way.

Most people, perhaps without realising it, are controlled by their emotions. They act with their emotions, not with their minds. In South America, there is a saying that goes *"No actués en caliente"* (roughly translated to "Don't act in the heat of the moment"), which applies to all aspects of our lives. Don't let your emotions control you. If you have to fire someone, don't do it because you are angry. We always see that in Hollywood movies - the nonsense boss who doesn't get what he wants and fires the first person who enters the room. While I'm sure it is based on a real-life boss, the reality is that no successful person is like that. I can't imagine Jeff Bezos doing it because Amazon shares dropped 1% that year, or Elon Musk after a failure to launch a rocket. One thing to add to all of this is that they respond to shareholders, and their perception of the CEO's ability to deal with his emotions is important for the future of the company.

While in our lives we don't have to deal with shareholders controlling each and every move we make, on the news, we always see people who cannot control their emotions. For example, how many times have you seen an act of road rage that escalated to the point that the police had to get involved? Those people aren't stable and allow their emotions to cloud their judgment. Most of the time, those very same people are the first who say that they regret what they did.

Keep your head cold, and your emotions in check.

7   Prioritise your tasks

You might think that those who accomplish a lot always have a thousand things on their plate, but the truth is that they focus on each task alone, and they dedicate enough time to see it through to the end. When they see that they can delegate a task, they get the best person possible to do it and allow them to tackle the problem. But this doesn't mean that they forget about it. On the contrary, they are back to check their progress in no time.

This is the secret of prioritization of tasks. You deal with one thing at a time, and then go on to the next thing. If you do everything at the same time, you won't finish anything. This applies to all aspects of your life. If you want to learn a new language, don't do it at the same time that you are driving to work. Focus on one task at a time. This doesn't mean that you cannot multitask. But if you try to cook and watch TV at the same time, you won't be able to do any of those to a satisfactory level.

Most of the time, the average person leaves their task to the last minute. They leave it because they focus on the most enjoyable task first, and then realize that they don't have enough time to do it, or leave it for the next day, and the tasks keep adding up. After a while, there are so many tasks that they can't do anything.

8   Focus your mind on improvement

At the end of the year, you will see lists like "The Books that I Loved This Year" (or something along those lines) published everywhere. If you ever take the time to read them, you will see that successful people read almost anything. From sci-fi to historical drama, they read every book that they find interesting.

This is something that always spiked my interest, and after trying it for a while, I realized why they do that, and it is because they want to be better at different things. We talked about how inspiration can come from different places, and that's the truth for them. They see every improvement, no matter how small, as a way to get to their goal. If they exercise (which all of them do), they see that every little bit of progress is far better than doing nothing and complaining.

If you aren't happy with your life and your situation, you can change it. Focus on what you can change, and confront what you can't. Nobody is going to knock on your door and say "here, you ordered success, sign here please". You must go out and face reality. You have it in you to do it.

We tend to believe that successful people all have high IQs (Intelligence Quotient), that destiny, God or the Universe decided that those special people are going to lead the way in several subjects, and break off the mould, or that they will tear down the walls of progress and make their own way.

Well… this is not the truth. Or at least, not the entire truth. According to several studies, there might be an advantage to not being a genius. While a certain level of IQ is obviously beneficial, you don't have to be a super genius like Einstein to achieve success.

When you study chess players, for example, your preconceptions will indicate that the higher the IQ, the better player they are. However, there have been several cases where the younger, inexperienced players (who felt like they didn't have as high an IQ as the more experienced player) always try new things or new plays and work twice as hard to master the basics. However, their rivals, being overconfident, didn't try as hard as they should have. This happens at every level of our lives, from business to sports. There is always the risk of not paying attention to a task, and more experienced people are prone to doing so. If you want to be successful, and become like the titans in business, always tackle problems with your full attention and deal with them with enough responsibility. It doesn't matter if you have done it 20 times in the past six years. Deal with it like it's the first time. Be strong, safe, honest, and direct.

Another factor that makes successful individuals stand out from the rest is their ability to comprehend and understand people and their attitudes. We previously talked about the power of interpersonal skills and how they impact a person's success, and because of this, we can infer that PQ (or 'people intelligence') is more important than IQ, at least when it comes to social skills and dealing with people.

If you ever asked yourself how well you work with others, and you took a long while to answer, then you probably aren't a people person, so you should focus on improving your skills and creating better bonds (which you are already doing if you have reached this point in the book!).

But once you realize that you can improve, and that 'Much to learn you still have' (like Master Yoda would say), the next step should be to become a master with 1o.ooo hours under your belt in any particular subject. Constant practice is the key to success, and if you want to become great, you have to dedicate several hours a week to reach that 10.000 hours mark.

Yes, it sounds like a lot of work, but that's what separates successful people from the rest. They made an effort to get there and become better, even when they were in pain. They have discipline, and they put in the hours that it takes to achieve mastery. They go beyond what is expected of them, so why wouldn't you?

The most successful people in the world embrace failure and use it as a starter point. Why? Because failing means that you can still learn, and learning is the best way to improve. It is in failure that we see our true self, and how we react to it will determine if it is a failure or just a minor setback.

When you fail, you will want to know what you did wrong. Write down your failures and critically evaluate what caused them. Create and brainstorm on ideas to avoid doing it again. Save those ideas, learn from them, and use them to turn your mistakes around. One quick way to do so is to find a mentor.

A close friend can help you see where you failed, make your ideas better, and push you in the right direction. They will hold you accountable, and you can write down a schedule to see the progress on your success, creating a timetable with several steps to push yourself. Adhere to that timetable, and you will see that this is one thing that you will have in common with the best in the industry. For example, Steve Jobs had Steve Wozniak, and they both created Apple together. Also, a mentor will keep you in check and warn you when you are veering outside your own path and will teach you from their experience in similar situations. This is an invaluable tool to become successful. They can be hard on you, but that doesn't matter. What truly matters is that they want success for you.

Body language is another important thing to know because your body will express more things that you can say with words. No matter how much you practice a specific subject, or how much your mentor pushes you, unless you can express and exude confidence with your body, nobody will take you seriously. All winners and losers have different body languages. From the alpha of the pack to the beta, they stand differently, and people thus treat them differently.

The true body language of a winner is to roll your shoulders back, open your chest, plant your feet, and always keep your head up. Look everyone in the eyes, and address them directly, with a safe an secure voice. This is the 'High Body Power' technique, commonly known as the technology that allows you to "take up space around you with your body"

If you master these skills, in time, no one will be able to stop you.

Chapter 8

How to be Interesting

In order to make new friends and to form long-lasting relationships, you have to do some work. We talked about the work that you have to put to express confidence and improve your own social skills, but I have more work for you to do. Don't look me at like that - you can do it. You already did the hardest part.

At this point in our trip together, you already have the consistency to implement a routine and maintain it. This is crucial, because being able to do it is an important tool from now on, and you will apply this consistency in the most important task ahead of you: becoming interesting.

This is not to say that you aren't already. I'm sure you are. We all are. But if you want to attract more people around you, and make them trust you, you have to show them what I already know about you: you are one in a million. Becoming interesting will allow people from all different parts of life to be drawn to you, and they will enjoy your company.

Being an active person is the first step and that is what you should should focus on for now. I previously mentioned that success won't come knocking at your door, and that's true for friends as well. Move out of your home and look for activities to do outside. For example, I enjoy reading at the park. Once a week, I go there with the book that I'm currently reading and stay there all day long. It is a deeply peaceful experience, and I would recommend it to anybody. While doing this, I met my current wife, because she was reading in the same tree that I used to read in. That got us talking about our preference in books, and one thing led to another. Needless to say, we are quite happy together, and that is all because I decided to get out and go outside. If you don't have a park nearby, you can always go to a coffee place or to your local library.

If you are lazy, however, and stay in your house watching TV all day, well, you aren't that interesting, to begin with. Go outside and experience the wild. It will do wonders for your health, both physically and mentally.

An active person is always doing something, whether it is learning a new language, training for a marathon, playing the guitar, or joining a new club. They always have stories and experiment with new things. Perhaps some aren't for them and they leave it after a while, but at least they tried to learn new things. They always have a story to tell, because they lived a lot. That's what you have to do.

I told you about optimism, and this is part of being interesting. If you have a pessimistic or cynic view on life, chances are that people won't enjoy being around you. After all, life itself is already hard enough without having someone telling us how bad it is every day. This does not mean that you must be absolutely happy go lucky and ignore the problems in the world, but rather to strike a balance between both these extremes. Don't go around constantly complaining about how bad a situation is, like rain, for example. Happy and interesting people are like magnets, and you will be more likable if you tackle life with passion and a desire for happiness.

Speaking of passion, here's a strong suggestion that I recommend: be passionate about any subject. For example, I am deeply passionate about video games and technology. I could talk for hours (and I did, just ask my wife) about how great Hideo Kojima is or how fantastic the concepts and technology behind self-driving cars are. My wife once told me a quote from Charles Bukowski:

Find what you love and let it kill you.

While Charles was a bit extreme, this doesn't mean that you have to die because of your passion (or at least, that's the interpretation that I got). It means that you have to immerse yourself in your passion and let it flow from and into you. Stay inside that passion, drink from it, absorb it, and above all, share it with every person that you meet. There is a certain magic in watching someone lose track of their time because they spent the last hour and a half talking about how much we need to save the whales, or about the last Star Wars movie. Their eyes shine and they start to move their hands in a way that it is contagious.

Passionate people are interesting, and being interesting is exactly what we want for you.

And to find what your passion is, what better way than to learn about every subject that you can? Read about anything that interests you, no matter the subject. Do you have an interest in the behind the scenes of movies? Then read a book about it. Do you want to learn a new language? Take a few classes or learn online. Don't stay in your couch all day doing nothing. When you go out and take classes or simply get out of the house, you will start meeting new people along the way, and that's the perfect way to create relationships. We talked about this before, but it deserves to be repeated - a shared interest is the best way to meet someone.

And learning about everything that interests you is the perfect way to have great conversation. I have a friend who is so well read that when you have a conversation about pretty much anything you can imagine, you can bet that he read about it. And it shows. It isn't like he's lying and doing it just to look interesting. On the contrary, he loves reading, going to museums, and listening to podcasts and great music. He loves so many things that for his birthday, the best gift we can give him is to take him to a library and tell that he can choose whatever book he wants. He always looks for one whose subject he doesn't fully understand or know yet.

For some people, reading that much is a bit weird. There are people that don't quite appreciate that quirk of his. He tried to hide away that part of him for years until he realized that he should let his weirdness shine. And that's an advice that I now use in my life, and I am now advising you to do the same. You have to stop being afraid to let people get to know your true self. Instead of being one among millions, be one in a million. Be different, be quirky, share your insights, and don't judge others when they do it, because you wouldn't want to be judged either. Break out of the mould that contains the normal personality that society says that we should have. Your experiences should be infused in this. Your activities should be absorbed in your personality and quirkiness. Believe me - whatever you think is weird, there are thousands of other people who do it too. Go find them, and be you with them, because they want someone like you to be. Let your weirdness pour out of you. Own your quirkiness!

And in these experiences, face your risks head-on. Always wanted to climb a mountain? Well, why not? Train and dedicate your time to do it, and then, go and climb it. Or, for example, perhaps you always wanted to travel alone. So, why don't you start saving money for that trip to America that you are always postponing? Push yourself out of your comfort zone and explore. Try new things. Remember, interesting people have interesting things to say, and they dare to do new things. Create a list of things to do in a year and cross off items as soon as you do them. And when you finish that list, do another. And another, and another.

Just like you are interesting (or trying your best to be), there are people around you that already have a rich life, full of experiences and activities. Why don't you ask them questions and really pay attention to what they say? If you show interest in the person next to you, they will love you for it, especially if you remember details from stories that they told you ages ago, since that means that you really listened. Practice the three nods that are mentioned earlier in the book, as well as your posture. Look at them in the eyes, and really listen to them attentively. Be curious, always have questions for them, assume that everyone is interesting and has something great to share, and regard everyone and everything as an opportunity to learn something new.

Start simple, ask them about hobbies, their future travel plans, their family, their experiences, etc. By doing so, you will get information on who they are and you can share your own experiences with them. Make sure that you pay attention to what they say. That's the key to becoming a better person - learning.

When it is your turn to talk about your recent trip to the Bahamas (or whatever place you want to visit), people will ask you details, like the weather, food, people, etc. And then, you may simply answer "yeah" or "nah", and that's it.

Wait, that's not right. You shouldn't do that. Expand your

story, give details, and tell them exactly how it was. Give them an image of what you experienced, and make them feel like they are there. This is basically something that humans have been doing since we learned to walk. Sharing stories and the power of words is the trait that connects us to our ancestors. If you are ever at a party, you will see that people gather around someone who is telling a good story. It is part of our genes because we all love a good story. If you want to become one of those, you can always take classes or watch oratory videos on youtube. You can see that some speakers do it when they have to deal with an audience. It is also part of what you learn if you want to do a standup routine. First, engage your audience by speaking about the setting (why, who, how, where and what), edit whatever boring stuff might have happened, and trim the fat of the story to keep your stories simple. Embellish it a bit if you think it is great for a joke or a pun, but don't go overboard, as it will be obvious when it is fake. Have a bit of conflict in your tale, and obviously, this struggle will lead to some change in the situation you are talking about. For example, if you are telling the story of how you got your car stolen, the car being stolen is your conflict, which leads to taking the bus, which is a change in your situation. If you add a moral to the story, or a lesson, then great. Oh, and if you haven't realized, this is basically the plot of most action movies and stories, like Star Wars, for example. Check it out.

Now, you've had some experiences and want to share them with the world. Which stories are you going to tell? That's an important question because your stories should make sense in the context of where you are. You can't tell a funny story at a funeral, for example (or you could, but it would be a little out of place). Think of three stories and be prepared to tell them at any time. Rotate them so people don't think that you are one trick pony. Take from your own experiences. Think about anecdotes from others that can be turned into good stories. And when it is your turn to tell them, use your face, hands, and anything else to get your point across.

If you are going to tell stories, tailor them to your audience. Let's say that you are talking with your grandmother who loves movies. In that case, you might tell her about the behind the scenes of Casablanca, but you might not want to talk to her about the Paris nightlife, as you know that she isn't really into those things. Always choose your stories according to your audience, and adapt to them to make them easier to understand. And if you are talking to someone for the first time, look at their body language to see if they are interested in your story or if they just want to get out of there.

And if the story doesn't work, tell jokes. Seriously, jokes work for everyone, and they have to be tailored to your audience as well. Don't oversell it, but practice your rhythm and tone. With due practice, you will get the tone perfectly. Or improvise, if that is your style. In improv classes, you have to think fast and better because your teacher will tell you that you have to act like a chicken and you better do it. That's my experience in improv classes, and they are so much fun because of that. They are great to help you lose your fear to deal with people and on top of hat, you will meet a lot of new people.

Conclusion

I used to be terrified of nobody paying attention to me. At any events where I had to speak with people that I didn't know, it made me think that my small talk sucked. I absolutely hated coffee meetings because they were nerve-wracking. And when I had the obligation to talk during team meetings, if I heard one single yawn from a co-worker, that would make me forget everything that I was going to say. To be completely honest, I was ashamed.

But one day, I realized that what I needed was passion. Passion for life, for food, for friends, for family, for everything. I'm not going to lie to you, because if you reached this point in the book, you know that I have always been honest with you. However, when I reached that point in life, I found out that I was depressed. The reasons why I was feeling like this weren't obvious for me at the time, but they certainly were after talking with my therapist for a couple of months. But she told me one thing that I never thought of before - to exercise. I was fit and wasn't overweight, and I didn't feel like I had to lose weight or anything like that. But at the time, I was unemployed and lived with my parents, and this was something that bothered me far more than I could explain or even realize.

I went to the gym in the same block as my parents' house, a place that I have never been before, and when I entered, I saw a man, about 50 years old, looking at me from a distance. I suddenly felt aware of my existence, aware that I hadn't shaved that week, that my hair was a bit untidy, and that I was very nervous entering there. Gyms, despite what we might think, are quite intimidating to someone that is socially awkward. I had to face the clerk and ask him about the prices and how much it cost to train there for a month or two, and I was really anxious. I hated talking to people, and for example, if I had to go to the bank, I always preferred to do it early, so I could deal with it quickly and go back home. The less I interacted with people, the better. Yeah, Rocks did wonders when I was a kid, but sadly, he passed away one or two years before, and I was dealing with it horribly.

The clerk told me that it was about $10 a week, or $30 for the entire month as a special offer for newcomers. I didn't think it was that expensive; however, my parents weren't financially well-off, so I thanked him and went out. Outside, the old man came close to me, and ask me if I wanted a job. Now, think about this: I was a socially awkward young man, and suddenly, a complete stranger asked me, out of nowhere, if I wanted a job. Don't lie - you would be scared too.

He realized that he looked a bit weird, so he presented himself. He had a pawn shop close to the gym and needed someone to help him. Well, I decided that I was going to talk to my parents and head there the next day. My father, of course, offered to go with me. The next day, we both go to see who this person was. He was in the shop and talked to us for hours. He told my father and I that he saw that I was trying to get in shape and that he wanted to help by giving me a small job. It wasn't going to have a great salary, just the bare minimum, but it could still help me get some money. I accepted and started that same day.

The old man told me his name was John, and went to the back of the shop, while I stayed in the counter to greet new customers. Then, that's when she entered. A girl with red hair, young and tall, who wanted to buy a hat for fer father's birthday. I was absolutely stunned, so I could barely mutter a few words and pointed to a small section that we had next to the counter, where all the hats and clothing were displayed. She smiled, and I was shocked. Why did she smile at me? Was she being polite? What about John, where was he? What was he doing in the back? But he wasn't anywhere to be seen, so I had to deal with it on my own. Sarah (that was her name) said that her father was an army veteran, but he always wanted to get better clothes. She wanted to offer him a hat, but her money was tight, so she had to look in pawn shops and thrifts stores.

I had no idea what to tell her, so I muttered and pointed to one that had everything that she wanted. The hat was $3, and she bought it with a smile on her face. John, who apparently was behind me during the entire exchange, asked me if I was nervous, and told me that if I wanted to talk, he was always there.

The first day came and went, and I went home. The week was really peaceful, and I went to the shop every day, even on Saturday. That day, John was going to close up the shop earlier and go watch a movie at the local theatre. He invited me to go with him. I said yes, so we went to his truck and headed to the theater which was on the outer limits of town. While he was driving, he asked me if there was something wrong with me, because he looked at my eyes and saw sadness.

At first, I didn't think that what he was doing was appropriate, but I realized that I wanted to talk. I didn't exactly know what I wanted to talk about, but I wanted to talk in general. So I told him the story that I told you at the beginning of this book, about my dog Rocks, how much I missed him, and the fact that I was starting to lose the confidence that he had given me. He looked at me for a while and said that he knew what I meant. We arrived at the theatre, parked, and entered. The movie was completely forgettable, and after it, we went to get some burgers. We started talking, and he took out a picture from his wallet. It was a woman, and she was smiling at the camera. He told me that she was his late wife that had sadly passed away a couple of months earlier.

All i could do was listen to him while he was talking about

her. He spoke about how much they loved each other, and how she helped him so much because he didn't have any friends before meeting her. She was his advisor and friend, especially when he needed it the most. I was shocked that he was telling me this because we only had known each other for a week, so I asked him why he was telling me that story. He said, and this is something that I cannot forget, that it was because he saw so much of him in me, and that he could help me if I wanted.

So from that day on, everyday that we spent together, we spoke about a lot of different things. He gave me a book as my birthday present, and it is a book that I still have to this day, twenty years later. He asked me to start exercising because he wanted me to get fitter. I started going to the gym almost religiously, every day after work to do some lifts, and then went back home. I did that for three years. Every time that I wanted to quit because it was too much work, he was there to tell me that I shouldn't.

He also asked me something that not even my therapist did: what was my passion? Why was I exercising? Was I doing it for me or for the therapist? During one of my sessions at the gym, I heard two guys talking about how they were going to get together and form a band one day. All they needed was a guitar player. I was curious about playing guitar because while I had never played any instrument, the guitar was one that I could see myself at least trying. I had a special taste for it, and when John and

120

I listened to his old records, I always played air guitar. I decided to save up some money and bought an old and really used guitar who had seen better days. John decided to take it to one of his friends that was a luthier who fixed it up for free.

My first classes were horrendous. I used a magazine that I found in the attic of my parent's house, and the chords made my fingers hurt. However, no matter how much pain I was in, I stuck to the plan: I was going to learn to play it because it helped me stay focused and allowed me to create my own music. Days led to months, and months led to a year. That's when I could say that I did it and had the talent for it. Playing the guitar allowed me to meet other people, and even form a short-lived Beatles tribute band. John was fascinated.

After a while, thanks to that band, I created a strong group of friends, one that I still have. That group led me to my first real job in IT, and that led me to where I am right now. John passed away years ago, but his message is the same that I say to you: You can do it, you are great and you have it in you to face absolutely everything that life throws at you.

I hope you enjoyed this book because I sure did enjoy writing it. Visit my website at http://jen.green as well and let's be in touch.

Go and take on the world.

We are waiting for you.